A Wild Thought...A Calm Mind

By: Tara Hoffman

First Printing, April 2021

CONTENTS

A WILD THOUGHT...A CALM MIND

THE PURPOSE OF THIS BOOK

I was driven to write this book because I saw a tragedy. When you see a tragedy, can you remain silent? I know I can't. I didn't witness a horrific slaughter of many people, a terrorist bomb that exploded in my hometown, or a young mid-pubescent boy walking into a school, opening his backpack and proceeding to slaughter his classmates and teachers with a gun he found in his parent's closet. But...the tragedy I witness now and for many years is the abandonment of the human spirit.

Many teachers and gurus have told me they believe that people are beginning to "wake up" to the fact that material goods are not the answer to finding their bliss. And they are beginning to pay attention to their spiritual lives. I hope that is correct but somehow I have not been witness to a spiritual awakening in this country. I see people going through the spiritual motions using their "training wheels" to prove to themselves and others that they are on the "spiritual path". I have critical news for them: the path to enlightenment has nothing to do with smiling and showing you are a kind person. Those behaviors will get you into the doors of heaven if that's where your path takes you but not to full enlightenment. For that goal, there is a much different path. It's simple but it's not easy.

I must warn you before we go further, that I'm very direct in my communication and my beliefs. I don't mean that as a challenge, insult or beratement to anyone....I just feel it's the most honest and true way to teach and I have appreciated it from my past teachers. I feel that honesty gives me something that I can hold close to my heart....that I never sweet-talked my way through the very important subject of spiritual evolution. Our spiritual development and walking our spiritual path is the most important thing in our lives...that's why we are here in this life to begin with. This world was created for us so that we could work out our karmic entanglements. Otherwise, how would we do so? The enlightened beings - whether they be Buddhas and Bodhisattvas, God or any of the Spiritual Deities who we pray to - are extremely kind and compassionate to allow us to work out our karma on this stage we call "Life on Earth".

So...the world was compassionately created for all of us ...not just humans. It was given to all beings whether they be human, animal, or any of the unseen spirits like wood nymphs, sprites and all beings most of us cannot see with the naked eye. But...we humans, in our arrogance and selfishness, see that this world belongs totally to us and we will rape and pillage it as we see fit. This is a huge tragedy against Mother Earth. That's why our planet is in such danger of ruin. Global warming and the decay of the ozone layer, the melting of the ice caps and destruction of polar and rain forest ecosystems are realities we should have addressed long ago but only recently have we begun to take these things seriously. And, some of our country's leaders don't even think this destruction really exists. I truly believe they mean well...but they are so obstructed from the truth by their greed that they cannot see what is right in front of them. When we are so focused on the physical world that we can see, touch, hear, smell and taste, we ignore the more important spiritual world. That is without a doubt the most sad state of affairs. Why?

The human mind is extremely creative and can create anything it wants. The problem: It is just as powerful to destroy. And it is doing so right now. We have no balance between the physical and spiritual world – internal and external. If all beings could live together peacefully and with some discipline, we would all be flourishing. Instead, we use animals as our beasts of burden, to gain wealth and to eat. We kill anything on this earth that is irritating to us. We are really the worst of dictators in our own little piece of the world.

In our backyards...we spray poison on weeds to kill them...did we ever think how lethal that substance can be to us? How about when it gets in our water supply? If we have gophers, we put poison in their homes to get rid of them. If birds leave their dirt on our walks, we do whatever we need to do to get rid of those "damn birds." Why do we do that? Why do we think that our lives are more important than the lives of others? I guarantee you that a bird's life is much more precious to HIM than OUR LIVES are to HIM. Everyone struggles for survival without bringing forth much altruism in our minds or hearts.

It's pretty obvious that if the world and its inhabitants continue on this destructive path, we will cease to exist in the same way we have become accustomed. When we cut down the rain forests to raise cattle, the beef industry is happy because they make a lot of money. Let's follow the progression. Less trees in the world means we have less oxygen to breathe. Less oxygen means people with lung issues will die. So...less people produce less carbon dioxide – the trees die even more. People eat more meat because they think more protein makes us stronger but really we become more unhealthy - and will die at an earlier age. Let's be smart and less short-sighted. Let's investigate how we can change this destructive downturn of the human mind. Do we think we are merely flesh and blood who have little control of our minds, bodies and environments? Or are we really much much more. I say we are more. I say we are everything.

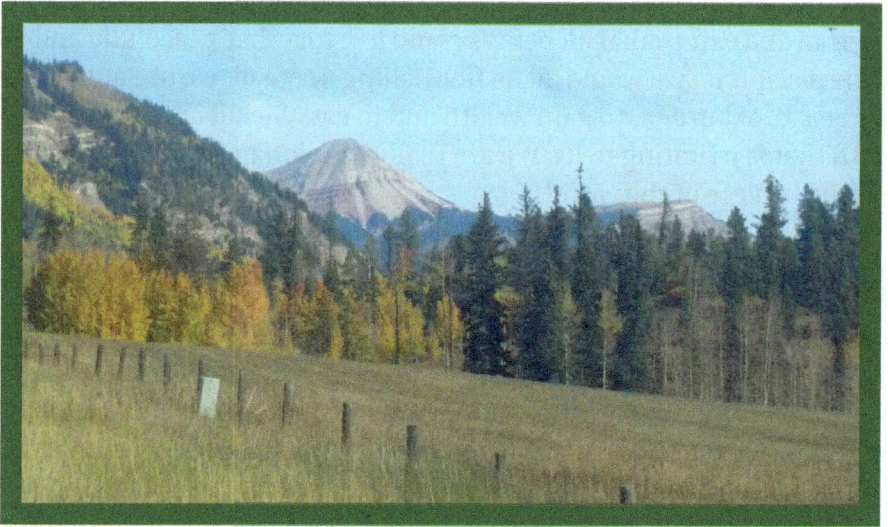

I am NOT what you think I am - YOU are what you think I am   - Buddha

Mrs. Miriam Kelly – My Mother

DEDICATION

This book is dedicated to someone who has supported me through thick and thin....to my Mother, Mrs. Miriam Kelly.

My mother is not related to me through flesh and blood but through the heart. I was once married to her son and even after my relationship with him ended, we remained close and our relationship is stronger than ever.

Although we loved each other very much, my biological Mother and I had a very rocky relationship. She has passed now but while she was on this planet, we worked hard to sort out a very tangled web. She always had my respect in every way and did all I could for her during our time together in this life.

My true mother - the one who is connected to me through our hearts of love and devotion - has always supported me through all my trials and tribulations. No matter how many messes I created for myself and no matter how many times I stumbled in my pursuits, she never doubted me even when I doubted myself. I cannot express how much she means to me. I love her with all my heart. She's definitely a Goddess in her own right and has been a strong support and comfort for her entire family and many friends.

As you will read later in this book, I left Scottsdale, Arizona after living there for over 20 years because I could no longer live in the city. Too many people; too much noise; and I just had to find a place to breathe - a place where I could observe nature in a natural environment. Mother encouraged me to make the months-long journey I made to find the perfect place to live and she came right along with me in spirit - demanding that I report to her every night to let her know where I was, that I was safe, and to share any tidbit from the day's travel that she may find interesting.

As I tirelessly traveled from state to state, I realized her love supported me every moment and that she was here on earth to carry on God's work. Through her prayers to the Blessed Mother, she helped save me from a horrific car accident that could have left me dead or worse.

I remember the accident as if it were yesterday. I actually rolled my car as a result of being hit from behind by one car and hit from the driver's side by another. The momentum of the collision sent me spinning out of control. Surprisingly, I was not afraid. Everything seemed to be in slow motion. I remember seeing two entities in front of me telling me I would be alright. One was my Beloved Spiritual Guide and the other was so familiar to me but I wasn't sure who she was. Somehow, I knew I would survive this accident and when the police pulled me out of the car, I had not a single scratch on me.

After calling my Mother to tell her of the accident, she told me right away the second entity was Mother Mary. She had been praying to the Blessed Mother for my safety during the trip across the western United States. As soon as she told me of her prayers, I realized that the Blessed Mother truly was one of the Deities who saved me. I am forever grateful for the Deities who intervened that day to protect me. Because of their kindness, I am here willing and able to help other beings find the True Nature of the Mind- whether they be human, animal, or those we cannot see with the naked eye.

Although my Mother and I live a distance from one another, there is no distance between our hearts. I speak with her several times a week and each time we converse, it is an interesting and heart-warming experience. I never question her love for me....it's just so obvious and I hope she knows that my love for her is also unconditional.

Without her sincere interest in wild animals and her delight in listening to my "wild animal stories" this book would not have been written. My dear Mother - how can I ever thank you for all you've done for me?

I dedicate this book to you, Mother, with Love.

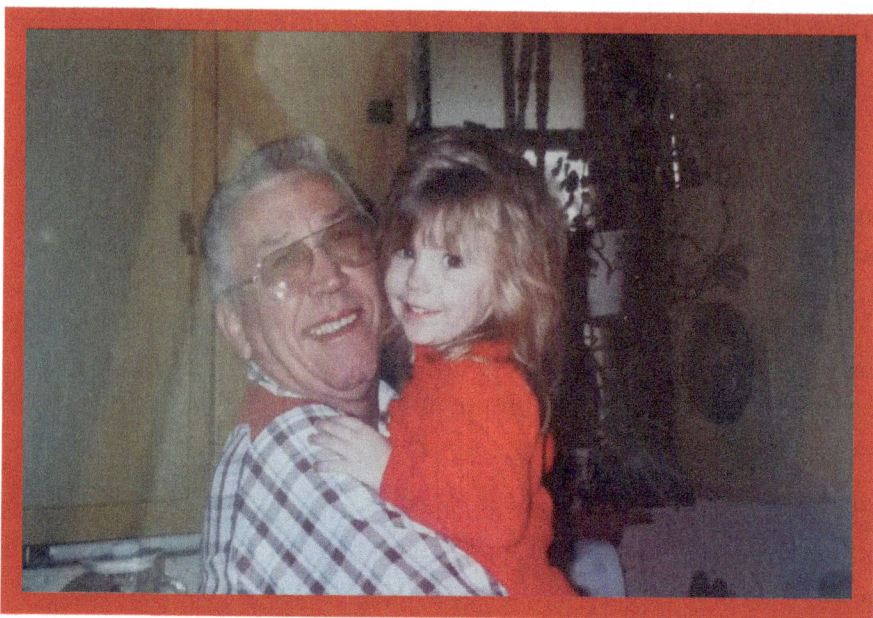

Angelique & Gramps (My Dad)

INSPIRATION

My daughter, Angelique, has been my inspiration in many ways from the time she was born. I wrote a book when I was pregnant with her – about all my experiences and thoughts when I carried her within me. This kid could not possibly have a thought of whether or not she was wanted. I planned my pregnancy down to the month and her father and I were so excited when we found out I would soon be a mother.

Angelique brought such joy to my life. I sat in wonder as I watched this little 3 year old frolicking in the yard – her blonde curly hair bouncing in the breeze. She was a free spirit - running through the dandelions in her bare feet. She reminded me of a beautiful, innocent wood fairy playing in the forest.

Many times she would help me "weed" the flower garden. When she took her nap, however, I would have to go out and replant the flowers she pulled out because she had a bit of trouble telling the weeds from the plants. Or...maybe she just saw all plants as equal and beautiful in their own right.

After a bit, I realized she saw things with a free mind - not twisting up her world with what's good and bad...right and wrong...weed or flower. It alerted me that she would be a very special being and how her life would unfold would be extremely interesting. She and I soon decided that all plants are beautiful and we welcomed all plants to grow in our yard and not discriminate one from another. What a powerful lesson to learn from a beautiful three-year old living being.

Angelique thought nothing of inviting her friend Mortimer the squirrel into the dining room to offer him a peanut. He would snatch it and bolt out the door to his nest. And there were the occasional birds who felt comfortable enough to follow us into the house. When the clover was blooming, I watched her frolicking through it in her bare feet...so many bees and rarely a sting. How did she do it?

I also experienced the most intense pain when she left my home at the age of 8 to live with her father. She had a special bond with him and after the divorce, she just needed time with him. I understood...but it hurt like hell. After she graduated high school she came to live in Phoenix – near me - so watching her grow up from a teen to an adult...was excruciating. She put herself in danger at times and occasionally ran with a rough crowd but I knew she needed to experience everything in life and she turned out to be an intelligent, beautiful, skillful, and amazing woman. I couldn't be more proud of her.

Since she lives back east and I'm in the west, we don't see each other nearly enough but we talk on the phone almost every day. During one conversation she floored me with a comment. I doubt that she realized how profound her statement really was when she replied, "Mom...when you're a kid all you ever want is to grow up. And now that I'm an adult, I really don't want the responsibility of it." That statement sunk right into my heart and I knew it was something I needed to hear.

I said to her, "I understand what you're going through. I don't want to be an adult with all the responsibility either. I want to remove all the unimportant crap from my life and just enjoy and experience. I want to be a kid again."

That conversation was an eye-opener. How often do we all get bogged down by all the worries and responsibilities that sap us of our life force and joy? This is a very simplified statement but it's important to remove all the unnecessary busy work from our lives. Few people are willing to set their feet on the spiritual path because they don't realize that there is so much more to life than going to work, cleaning the house, taking the kids to band practice, etc. We rarely take the time to really be present as our lives unfold and be aware of our spiritual progression. We need time to just BE...rather than DO. I think you all know what I'm talking about but it may seem like such a huge deal to tackle. For now, know that you can do it...one step at a time. That's the way enlightenment works...one step at a time...unloading one burden at a time until there are no more burdens or worries. We lighten our load and enlighten our mind.

I rely on Angelique so much for many things and we are extremely close. She's Rory Gilmore to my Lorelai - Mom and daughter as best friends. I can't imagine a world without her in it. Any employer she's worked for or a friend she's held close cherishes her. She's intuitive, spiritual and extremely dedicated to those she loves. She's my heart and soul and I will love and adore her for "Infinity". Her walk on the spiritual path is exciting and I'm with her every step of the way.

Thank you, Kid. You inspire me in so many ways. One of them was in the process of writing this book. YOU ARE TRULY THE LOVE OF MY LIFE!

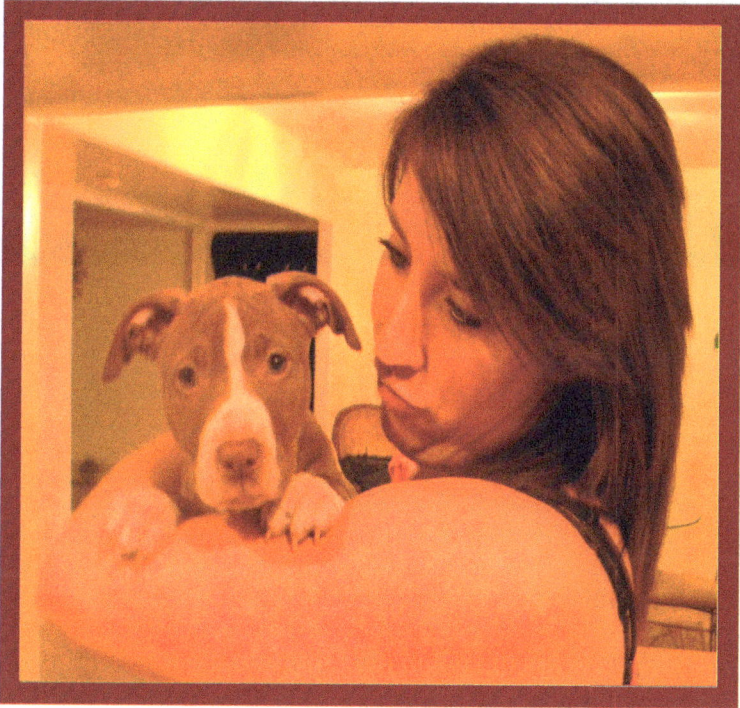

Angelique & Jenisis– Friends Forever

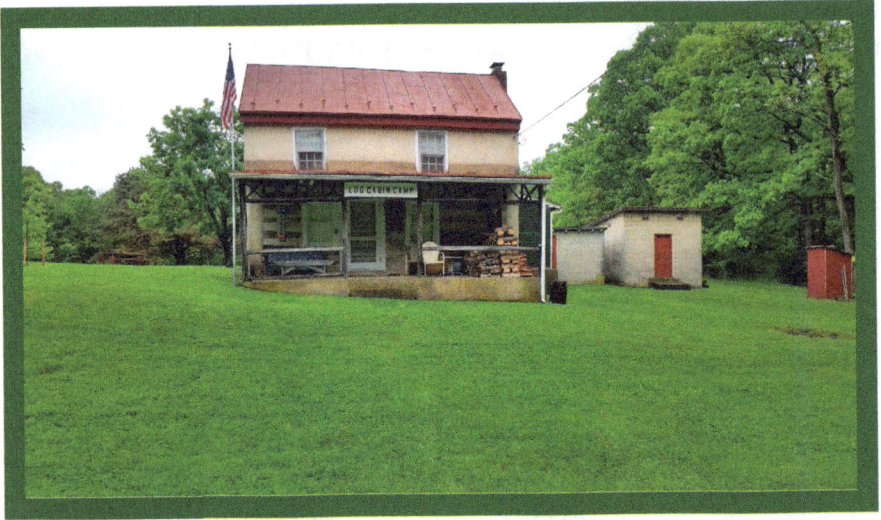

Family Retreat

BIRTH of a WRATHFUL BEING

HOW IT ALL BEGAN

I was just a kid...11 years old when my fairy tale life (or so I thought) came crumbling down.

I had just worked all day at my grandfather's farm. I was the fruit and vegetable stand salesperson - my first job. My grandfather was a teddy bear of a man. Pappy was the most gentle soul I ever met. I can remember living with him and my grandmother as a young child. Their farmhouse had an apartment on the second floor and my mom and dad lived there with me until my brother was born when I was 3 years old. When my parents would correct me, I would run down the stairs and crawl up on my Pappy's lap. He'd hug me and say, "What are they doing to my angel?" He was a great comfort to me and was a wonderful, wonderful man. Thinking back....I had several male figures in my life that were miraculous.

My dad's father, PaPa, was not the touchy/feely type, but he loved all his grandchildren ferociously. He was a very admirable man and strong beyond my own comprehension. I remember a story that my grandmother told me when my grandfather was courting her. He was out in the pasture cutting grass with a sickle...a big knife-type farm tool. He accidently cut his leg with the tool – a big gash in his leg but he kept on working so he could finish in time to go visit my grandmother. After he was finished working he walked to my grandmother's house (a good 10 miles away) which must have taken him hours - and sat down on her porch to share some lemonade. She looked at the blood on his pants leg and said, "Vic, your pants are all over blood. What happened on the way to my house?" He told her what happened and she was flabbergasted, "You walked all the way here after an injury with blood running down your leg? Are you insane?" He answered, "No....just in love." That did it for her. She married him and they remained married for 60 + years...till the day he died.

Papa was 100% honest - even when it was inconvenient. One day my grandmother invited me over for lunch and I was sitting patiently waiting for him to arrive. When he came in the door, he had a wallet in his hand. "Hurry up Milerd" (my grandmother's name was Mildred but he called her Milered..too funny). She said, "What's your hurry?" He explained, "I have to eat quick - gotta drop that wallet off to some guy on the other side of town."

He explained that when he came out of the paint store this morning, he saw a wallet laying in the gutter when he went to get in his car. He said he tracked down the owner and needed to return the wallet to him. There was a sizable amount of money inside and the owner would be hurting pretty bad if he didn't get the wallet back. I said to him, "Papa...did anyone see you pick up the wallet? What makes you think you have to return it?" (I was testing him). He looked very intently into my eyes and said, "If there's one thing I've learned, it's that we should always live a life of integrity." "What does integrity mean to you, PaPa?" His gaze never left me and then he said, "It's doing the right thing – no matter who's looking– even if no one is looking". I got his message and never forgot it. I've noticed that when I lived my life as he did, my life was peaceful and wonderful. Now I know that the wisdom I learned from my Grandfather was only the beginning of my many lessons. There was more to realize on my path.....much more.

Because of my grandfathers, I learned how to live a virtuous life and one of kindness to others. There were times that my human nature got the best of me but I realized that our negative thoughts, words, and actions only come back to bite us. The more negative thoughts we have - the more negative words we use and the more negative actions we take. There's no doubt about that. A wise Teacher once said to me, "When you spit poison, just remember that it was first in your own mouth." The picture of that in my mind wasn't a pretty one so I tried to avoid the dark side....although I walked through it from time to time. Let's be honest.

So, I had one grandfather with unbelievable integrity and one that was so gentle and loving. Could this have been my own manifestation of the balance between wisdom and compassion....hmm.

My father was a tough guy on the outside and soft and mushy on the inside. He loved to have a good time and his laugh was infectious. I think I inherited that from him. Laughter is such a good medicine - don't you think? Many of us in this world today lack the ability to feel joy. Some of the craziest things strike me funny. Like when the squirrels jump onto the table I have on my porch and try to get the peanut jar open. I keep peanuts in a jar that twists shut - not easy to open even for me but somehow those little guys get that top off. It makes me roar with laughter. They never give up and are skillful and quite the comedy act.

For the female figures in my life: My dad's mother, Ma, was amazing. She was strong, feminine, beautiful, and loving. You couldn't walk into her house without eating. Her mantra was "Feed 'em!" I loved her so much and she and Papa had a really good relationship – each playing their own roles very nicely. My brother and I spent a lot of time with them at the family's cabin in the beautiful, lush Appalachian mountains. We all spent so many weekends and holidays up there – 100 acres of wooded land...wow. I didn't appreciate it so much then but I absolutely do now.

My mom's mother, Nan Nan was a cold, bland woman. I knew she loved me but boy...it was so hard to tell. She was a farmer's wife and did a great job of it - cooking amazing meals and canning and freezing vegetables and fruits for winter. And her mother – my great grandmother, Mi Mi - she was a tough bird too but had a soft spot in her heart for me. When she made fresh pies, I got my own little peach turnovers, etc. I was with both of them non-stop from the time school ended for the summer until it began again in the fall and I learned some very useful skills from them.

My mother was pretty much a clone of her mother and grandmother. Although, luckily for us kids, she was a little softer. But what I remember about her the most was her ability to work from sunup to sunset. She worked a job and then came home to work like crazy in the house and take care of two kids. I think I get my tenacity from her.

She did produce some fun for my brother and I during our childhoods but from the time she divorced my dad (when I was age 11) and remarried, I remember a woman who was obviously repressed by her new husband and soured by the promises he failed to keep to her. He promised her money and happiness. The first she got. The second...not so much.

Like I said, I had some strong, honorable male figures in my life and some unhappy, hard working women in my lineage. Thankfully, I had two female role models (Ma) and her daughter - my Aunt Ruth) who gave me hope for my sanity and happiness. They were the ones who showed me what being a woman is all about. They worked hard – but not relentlessly to forget about misery and disappointments. They were soft and loving and demonstrative which I didn't get from the other females in my life. So -I leaned on Ma and Aunt Ruth to show me the ropes.

These people in my family were my foundation and in their own ways, they were good people who loved my brother and me but they didn't quite prepare me for what happened on that Saturday afternoon when my mom told me she and my dad were getting a divorce. At that moment, I became the woman of the house and took on the caring role for my dad and my brother.

I was only 11 years old and so much responsibility fell on my shoulders. My father tried to parent us but my brother and I were left unsupervised most of the time. So I became the caretaker for a child 3 years younger than me. After all...if I didn't do it, who would?

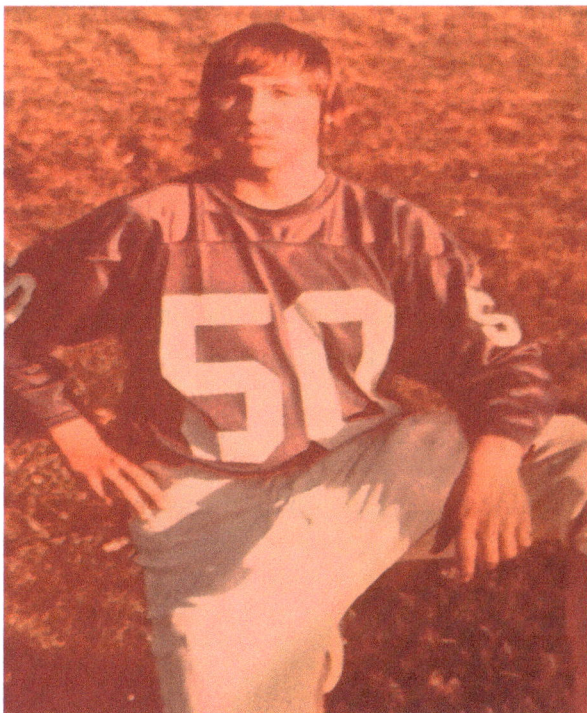

Mervie - My Brother

Both my brother, Mervie and I were so mad at my mom for breaking up our family. We were too young to understand the complicated human life. We were hurt and felt that our mother really didn't love us since she threw us aside for a man we had no intention of caring for. We didn't realize her divorce from our dad had nothing to do with us or her love for us but we were pissed and vengeful so we decided to stay with our dad rather than live with her.

My dad maintained the home but he was very sad after the divorce and used alcohol to numb the pain. I worked hard to get good grades in school, participate in some extra-curricular activities, cook dinner for my brother and I and take care of the house and shopping. Needless to say, taking all of this on was a huge burden for me and one I carried through most of my life. In the long run, however, it enabled me to realize that if I could take care of my dad and brother, school responsibilities and activities....and still have a teenager's life, I could do anything.

I kind of got the hang of things after the first several painful years. Mervie and I looked out for each other. We had lots of adventures together and between my brother's best friend, Brian, and the two Hoffman kids, we were a force to be reckoned with. The two boys were full of zest and vigor and played a lot of pranks on the neighbors. One summer night they knocked on my bedroom window and begged me to come out with them. They had something to show me.

I stepped out of my window and we ran up to the neighbor's house. What they didn't tell me was that they had set off a saltpeter bomb in the neighbor's driveway. Saltpeter mixed with sugar is not dangerous but it does create a stinky, smokey result when lit.

When we arrived at the neighbor's house, the bomb was still smoking and we laughed with glee until a gunshot pierced the night air. It was the neighbor who obviously saw (and smelled) what the two boys had done. We didn't realize the neighbor was shooting over our heads. We thought we were goners so we ran like the wind across the road and into my grandfather's peach orchard. I was so scared that I forgot about a leach field (a kind of rural sewer ditch) of the neighbor's and fell right into it. Oh My Gosh...I was knee deep in sewer smelling goo but I picked myself up and ran through the orchards...in my bare feet I might add.

As I ran, I could hear Brian and Mervie laughing loudly as they ran ahead of me. They were scared but exhilarated. I was just scared and threatened them with bodily harm if they ever involved me again with such craziness. Secretly, I thought they were amazing - adventurous, creative and very annoying...an interesting combination for teenage boys.

When we both grew a little older - I was 19 and Mervie was 16, he introduced me to his first girlfriend. It was then that I realized Mervie was a sensitive, non-judgmental, and beautiful young man. But it didn't last long. Mervie was just 16 when he died. At that point, my parents were beyond heartbroken. My dad's world went from sad to desperate. He had just begun to date a lady named Shirl and he had a glimpse of hope in his eyes when he gazed at her. He loved Shirl with all his heart and was happy again until that fateful Saturday.

Mervie was playing basketball at the neighbor's house when he collapsed. The neighbor kids ran to get my dad but when he arrived, my brother was already gone. Although it wasn't logical, my dad blamed himself. He felt that if he had arrived earlier, he could have saved his son. Our family doctor confirmed that there was no definitive cause of death-even after the autopsy and there was nothing my dad could have done to save him. But despair knows no logic and Dad held that pain until the day he died. Why did my brother die? To this day I have no idea.

This scenario began another sad chapter in the lives of my parents and me. They were in pain but I got pissed. At the funeral, I asked our church Pastor why God would take a young boy away from his family and his life at the age of 16. The answer I received was unacceptable. The pastor answered, "God must have needed little angels." I got so angry that I yelled at him and told him that was the most ridiculous answer I had ever heard. Needless to say, my Mother was mortified at my behavior. I took note that she reacted more to what I said than considering that maybe I had a point. This incident put me on the path....the path for spiritual realization – the quest for the **TRUTH.**

RELIGION

Have you ever seen the movie "Kundun"? It is the life story of His Holiness the Dalai Lama - from the time he was recognized until he and other Tibetans settled in northern India to escape the atrocity of China's invasion of their country.

There are so many moments in that movie that show the violence that arose because of the Chinese government's disregard for the Tibetan people. There was one scene I will never forget. The leader of China at the time - Mao Tse Tung - was meeting with HH the Dalai Lama and Mao looked at His Holiness and said, "There is one thing I want to tell you.....religion is poison." Well...you can imagine how His Holiness reacted to that statement. After all, he was the spiritual leader of the Buddhist people and also a leader of the Tibetan government. His Holiness did not respond. What Could he say to a person who believes that his spiritual life is unimportant and only relies on the physical world for his contentment?

I have the greatest respect for His Holiness - he is a living Buddha but on a different scale I believe that religion serves as a stepping stone - not the final destination to one's spiritual enlightenment.

The purpose of any religion is to keep people on a positive path. That is a very great benefit if our goal in life is to remain on a positive note. If we attend church and feel that we are progressing nicely through our lives, giving to others and raising our children to be "good people", then religions are the best route to take. We will live a good life and go to heaven or to whatever place we believe we will go after this life is over. For this path, religion is the greatest path.

However, walking a religious path will only take us so far. It's like training wheels on a bicycle. They keep you safe and happy for as long as you need them but when you're ready to ride a two-wheeler, you need to take the training wheels off. It's not to say that religious beliefs are good or bad, they are just what was needed at the time. For those people who come to this life to walk a path to full enlightenment, the training wheels have to come off.

Jesus Christ and the Buddha definitely understood how to become enlightened and they each taught those aspects in their own doctrine and in their own way. However, the Bible and the Sutras weren't even put to paper until many years after the Buddha and Jesus Christ left their physical bodies and moved to their spiritual forms. There is historical evidence that human religious leaders stepped in afterwards and changed things around a bit. The teachings of the Buddha and Jesus Christ were altered from what was originally taught. I'll say it again - "The audacity and arrogance of certain groups of human beings to control the masses is unbelievable." But..it happens all the time. That's why we have to be careful about what religious rules we follow because we cannot be sure of whether or not it is wisdom imparted to us from Enlightened beings or something that was inserted later by a group of our peers. Wisdom cannot be faked so ask your heart. If your heart tells you what you are learning is wisdom, then accept it. If it doesn't make any sense to you, discard it.

I have studied Christianity, Buddhism and New Age philosophy so far in this life. Christians are happy to go to Heaven after they die. New Age people aspire to exist in the 10th dimension and see auras. Buddhists aspire to enlightenment - mostly to escape their "negative karma" they have created after living many lifetimes.

Christians believe they will live in Heaven for eternity after their physical life on earth ends. Buddhists believe that life in the heavens will last for a long time and bring them limitless bliss. But it is not permanent and after a period of time, one will fall from the heavens. So the question is: after we die, how long do we live in heaven? The Christian and Buddhist texts oppose one another. So...who is right? Is there really a "right" and "wrong" at all?

Buddhism teaches us that life is suffering. Some beings suffer more than others as a result of the fluctuation of the mind and their karmic bank. There is an end to suffering...which is enlightenment. But what is the process that frees us from suffering? Buddhist texts say it is to keep our karma positive and light. But how do we do that? I've read many Buddhist teachings and spent time with many high Buddhist Masters -

some of whom are already enlightened. But nowhere did I find a step-by-step method on exactly HOW to become enlightened.

My path has been to remove the training wheels....altogether and follow the life and teachings of Prince Sidhartha who became Shakymuni Buddha. He realized the path to enlightenment is not in extremes, but in the Middle Path - the path of least resistance. After he led a life of luxury as a prince, he went into the forest and led a life of poverty as an ascetic. It was at his most vulnerable moment, when he almost died of starvation, that he realized the answer to enlightenment was by walking the Middle Path - not too loose and not too tight....not extreme.

I can assure you I have the highest respect for all the religions of the world. However, I'm presenting these ideas by looking behind the curtain - not just accepting what is seen. Both the Buddha and Jesus Christ had mankind's best interest at heart but there is evidence that certain groups manipulated the teachings after these Great Teachers left their physical bodies and some teachings were changed by those in power to control the masses.

If our goal is for full enlightenment, in my experience, there is only one way. That is to Free the Mind. Think about it...ENLIGHTENMENT is to LIGHTEN the mind. How do we do that? It's pretty obvious that negative thoughts are heavy. Think about a time when you were very sad and depressed. Didn't you feel heavy with no motivation to do anything other than sit and sulk? Yes...we have all been there. However, what you may not be aware of is that positive thoughts also have weight. So...how do we lighten the mind?

It's a simple method but it's not easy to do.

Clark and the Boys

WILD ANIMALS

We human beings feel that animals are beneath us. Some people even feel it's OK to use animals for their entertainment, for their meal and just as a way of taking out their anger onto another being. In my experience, wild animals are far more evolved than humans. Of course they don't have a complicated brain...and that's why I say they are more evolved spiritually. This book was written as a way of sharing my experiences and how these amazing animals and birds led me down the path of lightening the Mind. While a human mind is very heavy with obligations, responsibilities, etc., an animal's mind is light.

Wild animals are always aware...always in the moment. If not, they will be killed by a predator. They are very in touch with their powers of sense and intuition and they know who will love them and who will hurt them. They have very few desires - a little food and shelter is all they ask for and some have no shelter at all.

I have learned so much from every animal I've created a relationship with. When one spends time building relationships with wild animals, the rewards are immeasurable. Free the Mind was created from observing them and beholding the way they interact with one another and with me. They ask for little food and in return, they give back so much. I am forever in debt to all my animal friends in hopes that other people will understand them a bit better so that all the harshness bestowed upon them by human beings stops. I also hope this book will open your eyes about how animals are treated in this world. No matter how much we speak about loving thy neighbor and being a "good person", all of this practice in kindness is futile if we abuse our pets or disregard the lives of our wild animal neighbors. If we just give them a chance, they can bring such goodness into our lives. I, for one, am very blessed because I love them with all my heart....and they love me as well.

What I learned in general from wild animals: How to lighten the mind - to let go & be free.

SCOTTSDALE

Scottsdale, Arizona is great for anything you want to experience - from malls to restaurants, to golf courses to great entertainment. Lots of wealth, business, entertainment, etc. - much like other large cities. Scottsdale is good for staying busy but not so good for spiritual growth. While I was there, I made the best of it. My front yard consisted of native cactus and palm trees. However, my backyard was just the opposite. It was lush and green - like an east coast lawn.

My life in Scottsdale was very quiet and low-key. I had a home office and worked for a pharmaceutical company from home. I had a big garden and rarely bought any vegetables from the grocery store. In fact, I shared my veggies with human friends as well as my rabbit and squirrel friends...there was plenty for everyone.

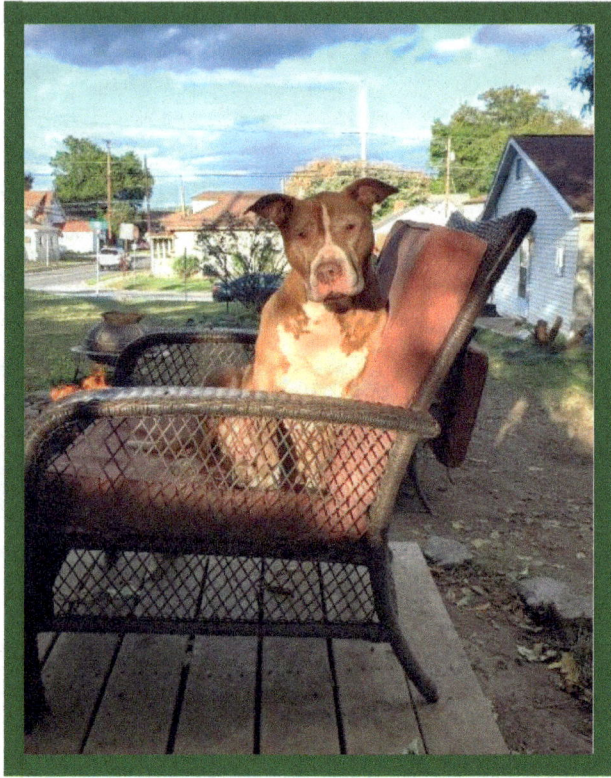

Jenisis – She Took My Heart for Ransom

JENISIS

I could easily write an entire book about Jenisis – my daughter's pitbull. The propaganda about pit bulls and the way people buy into that rubbish is just ridiculous. I don't doubt that a dog who is built like a tank and as protective as a big brother would have the capability of doing harm to a human. But...any other dog (or any animal for that matter) could do the same. Pitbulls are extremely protective and I admired that in Jenisis but she was mostly all talk and not much action – although I don't doubt that she would rise to the occasion if anyone put her family in danger. She just wanted to make sure we were safe and I honored her for that trait. She would have given her life for us in a New York minute.

There was a time when my daughter, Angelique, and Jenisis came to live with me. Jenisis was still very young and I was concerned that I would regret having a puppy in my house. Would my rugs get chewed up and would there be urine all over the floor? You know...a normal puppy.

Very obviously, it was a time for all three of us girls to be together and I love Angelique more than words can express so I welcomed both of them into my home and we had a great time together....interesting at times...AND great.

Physically, Jenisis came in the form of a dog but she was a true Deity spiritually. She came to my daughter as a gift from a former friend and she took both mine and Angelique's hearts for ransome. Never have I been able to see the true nature of a being so clearly.

Jenisis soon put my fears about a chewed-up house to rest. She was a dream. She has a true sense of awareness and wisdom that I've not seen in a pet before. I knew then that there was something special about her but couldn't quite put my finger on it.

Since I was working as a computer technician from home, it was a perfect situation for Jenisis. She would roam around the back yard (almost an acre of horse property which was rare in the middle of the city) and lay in the green grass...chasing birds, ground squirrels and rabbits trying to steal some vegetables from my garden. Once in a while she would come into the house and wander into my home office - just checking to see what I was up to. On the way out to the back yard (I always left my back door open) she would have a drink of water from her bowl or a quick snack. Then....back out to patrol the yard and make sure there were no intruders.

One day I heard rattling in her food bowl and thought she had come in quietly to get a snack...but then I heard a ruckus in the kitchen...barking and paws skating around the kitchen floor. I walked out to see a bird called a Thrasher flying out the door. I am very familiar with Thrashers.

They're fascinating. Their red eyes are a bit creepy, but they're smart and bold well beyond their size. I loved them...just as I do all wild animals and birds.

Apparently, a Thrasher had flown into the kitchen and had stolen a morsel of Jenisis' food. Well...as far as Jenisis was concerned, that was a capital offense. She had no intention of sharing her food. From that moment on...the Thrashers and Jenisis had an ongoing contest of wits...one would lure her into the lower end of the yard and the other would steal some food. I saw this clearly and the interesting thing was....so did Jenisis.

There was a bowl of peanuts sitting on my kitchen counter and I'd throw them to the ground squirrels as they came onto the porch. The Thrashers had different ideas. They would fly into the kitchen, walk onto the counter and help themselves. Once I caught them stealing mac and cheese that had spilled onto the kitchen counter. Those birds felt right at home and did help themselves. By the time these birds grabbed a delicious morsel, the pit bull patrol was scurrying through the kitchen - chasing the intruder out the door. This went on all day long and was hysterical to say the least.

Jenisis was also very well behaved and only caused me any real angst when she insisted on visiting the two pitbulls next door. A 6-foot cinder block wall separated Jenisis from her peers and she wanted to go visit them. When this dog was on a mission, she wouldn't let go until she succeeded. Morning after morning, she would try to scale the wall and get to the other side when she heard her friends come outside for their morning constitution.

Many mornings I would run into the yard in my pajamas - screaming for her to get down from the wall. Several times she came very close to jumping over to the other side and one morning I found her teetering on top of the wall on her belly ready to dive over to the other side. Luckily, my screaming distracted her long enough for me to grab her. She would become bashful and remorseful after her attempts but would try again when the occasion presented itself. In fact, Angelique and I started piling furniture and "things" next to the wall so she wasn't able to scale it. But...she was an agile warrior and not easily dissuaded from what she wanted and she never really gave up.

Angelique and Jenisis have a bond that cannot be broken. The pit loves me but nothing could come between her and my daughter. They are together...and I mean together. Even in sleep.

Sleeping with another individual is always a unique experience but never have I beheld a more beautiful sleeping arrangement than Angelique has with Jenisis. The pit would sleep totally submerged in blankets. I call her "the pit mole". When the sun comes up...I'm up so early in the morning I would open the door to Angelique's bedroom very quietly and say..."Jenisis...do you wanna go outside?" This crazy dog would crawl to the end of the bed under the covers and slide out the bottom part of the bed. Of course....having tucked in sheets and blankets was an impossible goal with "the pit mole" around! She would go outside and do her business and then most times would go right back to bed. She would walk up to the side of the bed where Angelique was facing, my daughter would lift up the covers, and Jenisis would submerge again. The two of them were like a finely-oiled, cohabitating sleep machine.

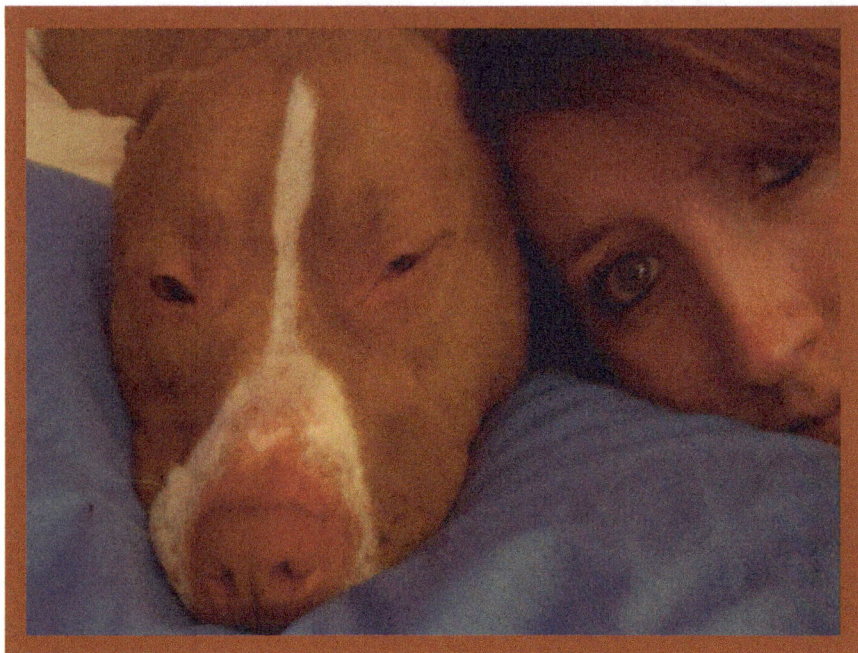

Observing Angelique and Jenisis together showed me that a relationship between human and animal could be very intimate. The life that they orchestrated for themselves created an unbreakable bond - not to be diminished by time and space. To this day the strong bond and love these two have for one another is unbreakable.

My special times with Jenisis revolved around food. Since my household has been vegetarian for 30 years, there are many meals that start out with a stir fry of vegetables. Since I had a bountiful garden, there were lots and lots of ingredients for those stir frys. When dinner time came, I'd say to Jenisis, "It's veggie time!" She would jump to her feet and stand between the counter and the stove...where the vegetables may possibly drop to the floor....and a few ALWAYS dropped to the floor. Luckily, I had a cleaner upper ready to pounce into action. That was our time...cooking and we both enjoyed it immensely. I still think of her when I drop food on the floor.

One of our favorite family outings was to go to our summer retreat camp in the Appalachian Mountains. There Jenisis and I took hikes, went swimming and hung out in the shade of the big pine tree. I spent much of my childhood up at that cabin (which was owned by the entire Hoffman family) and it was my joy to share it with one of my favorite beings.

The Pit Mole

Even though the miles separate us, Jenisis and I often talk over the phone and let her know I love her and our hearts are forever intertwined. Never have I been able to see so clearly that the spiritual essence of a being has nothing to do with their form. To me...Jenisis was and still is a powerful, loving Goddess - possessing the wisdom of the Buddhas and Bodhisattvas. She is my daughter's protector and, believe me, she takes her job very seriously.

What I learned from Jenisis: Unconditional Love and Devotion

Rabbit Friends Feasting on Apples

WILD ANIMALS in SCOTTSDALE

The Scottsdale backyard was filled with wild friends who came to snack on my offerings. Ground squirrels loved the peanuts, rabbits came for the carrots and apples, quail came for the bread and seeds, and the hawks came for all of them. Nature taking its course doesn't bother me too much except that I never want to see an animal harmed. Predators also have to eat to survive; however, watching humans unleashing their wrath on wild animals infuriates me. I understand all too well what Jane Goodall was feeling when poachers came into her gorilla community - guns blastin'.

In the animal kingdom, change is not accepted readily. When something is different or something just FEELS different to animals and birds, they respond with extreme caution. These intuitive beings are extremely in tune with their environment so one little difference brings on a fight or flight response...usually flight.

We've all seen animal mothers protecting their young – bears will attack humans to keep their cubs out of harm's way; mother rabbits lead a predator away from their young; and I've seen two adult hawks draw blood on each other because one female who was not part of the colony got too close to the young one. Mothers protecting their young is a universal instinct which ultimately helps the species to survive. Animals tend to band together and altruistically protect their community from harm. When I witness it, it's beautiful.

The animal kingdom's fear of predators is not their only danger. Animals and birds have to be very cautious about the human realm. Many humans are not kind to them and treat them as nuisances. Strange...basically, I find that the arrogance and lack of compassion on the part of many humans is a nuisance. In fact, I rarely become annoyed with a wild being. They are just following their instincts. As you will come to realize after reading my book, I have been around many wild animals and none have shown me any aggression.

I have walked out into a herd of ten huge mule deer bucks every day – their antlers between 8 and 12 points - offering them corn and apples in the middle of winter. One day as I stood among them, I became aware that they were surrounding me. There was a lot of artillery on those heads. They could have trampled me and taken all my offerings but they didn't. They were grateful that I was sharing some food during a long winter in Colorado. People told me deer get very aggressive in mating season...that may be true but I would walk through my herd and no one ever showed me anything but love.

I had a community of 50 + turkeys I was friends with in Dolores and I walked among them to offer popcorn. Although the males weren't exactly tolerant of younger males, never did they show me aggression. Friends would tell me to be careful because wild turkeys can be very mean. I believe them because I saw five of them chase off a coyote. But they were kind to me.

My point here is that animals are extremely intuitive and they are aware of who they can trust. I'm not sure if they feel love like humans do but they are extremely humble with me and very appreciative of my caring for them. If you respect wild animals and mean them no harm, it is rare for them to harm you. In general, they don't care to be around humans so they don't make a move to become friends. It takes a lot of time and patience (and food offerings) to gain their trust but it's so worth it.

Wild animals live by their gut...not their conceptual thinking. They react to their environment and for the most part, don't have a plan for their lives. They rely almost totally on their instincts. Humans are another story, however. We have mostly lost track of our basic instincts and have let our rational mind take over our existence. That's too bad for us. Unfortunately, we are not following our hearts as much as we should and in the long run, it makes us miserable. The great thing about the human realm is that when there is a disaster (as we have experienced recently) humans will band together...and that's a beautiful thing.

Scottsdale is a great place to live if you like outdoor activities. The summers are pretty hot but from October to June the weather is heavenly. It was kind of nice to speak with my family back east on Christmas day and let them know I was dangling my feet in the pool. I usually begin the days outside on the porch with Spencer the hummingbird and the rest of the brood of animals and birds...and any reptile who lives in the backyard. I love being with them when they are eating...they relish the food. The birds eat and drink and then take a bath. Watching birds in a bird bath is a joyful experience. There was a contractor who came to my house to give an estimate for house painting and the birds were bathing in the bird bath. I immediately smiled and said..."I don't know what it is about the birds taking a bath but it always gives my spirit a lift." He smiled and said to me, "That's because you experience joy....most people have lost that these days."

I'll never forget what he said because he opened up a whole can of worms that is both exhilarating and disturbing. Have we really lost our ability to feel joy? I think many of us have – especially those of us in our golden years – after raising our children and feeling that society really doesn't want or need us anymore. I myself have felt those dangerous pangs and let me say this loud and clear to others who have had that feeling...JUST BECAUSE WE ARE OLDER IN YEARS SURELY DOESN'T MEAN WE ARE OF NO USE TO THIS WORLD....LET'S GET REAL! IN FACT, JUST THE OPPOSITE IS TRUE.

Have we forgotten how important elders were in the indigenous cultures? What about the wisdom that we have gained from our years on earth? I watch my deer herd pay the utmost respect to the elders. The young males are very careful not to mess with the older males or females – or they get a kick in the behind (literally).

Human children are busy with school and having "fun"...whatever that is for them. The young adults are working feverishly on their careers and finding the spouse of their dreams. Then there is marriage and raising children. All of those things keep human beings extremely busy and unaware. It's not until we reach our golden years - when our children are grown and we parents only worry about them half the time, that we actually have some moments to get to know ourselves, explore who we are and what we want, and have time to JUST BE. It is then that we hopefully explore our spiritual path. After all....pursuing our spiritual growth is why we came to this planet. Trust me...we didn't come here to work for (and get kicked around by) a corporation. We came to work out our karma and find a way to reveal our spiritual nature that will never die...but will go on and on until we become enlightened.

The hindrances to our spiritual growth are being too busy and going along with society's "rules" even if they make no sense at all. Remember- if we are too busy working, getting married, having children, etc. and are not keeping our eye on the ball, our society can really pull a fast one on us. We need to be present, have our own minds, and most of all....be aware so we can tap into our innate wisdom no matter what obstacles we encounter.

I can remember my father saying to me that no one in his family (before me) had gone to college. He went on to explain that all the men in the family were blue collar workers and that's what he would do. I realized even at that young age that he was following suit. His father did it as did his father before him. But the society my Grandfather lived in was different from the one today. Heck...his father came straight off the boat from Germany so I imagine the Hoffman clan's customs and ideas came from Europe. Do they make sense today? Many don't. Did they ever make sense? We'll put a pin in that.

From the time we are born, our culture puts its imprint upon us. All our lives we learn the "right" thing to do and say and we strive to be "good" people. But who decides what is "right and wrong"or "good and bad?" It's the society. And what shapes society? Our peers – no "better or worse" than we are.

Our religious groups also make rules within our society on what is good and bad...right and wrong. I do understand why the religious groups put all the rules together...to keep people on the "right and good path". But then...the right and good path is different with any society you will encounter. There are few universal rules that most religious groups attest to like No Killing, No Lying, No Stealing,....etc. But those rules are just in the human realm. The animal realm and other realms (oh yes...there are many realms in this universe) don't hold human rules as gospel. In fact, the animal realm has no rules that oppose killing or stealing....or coveting thy neighbor's wife. They are much freer than we humans. Better or worse? I say...neither better nor worse.

When I was a freshman in college, I took a course in Anthropology and that class opened my eyes. We examined the customs and practices of many people from many different cultures. Many practices from different cultures conflicted with our own. We also examined the life of Jesus Christ and learned that there were many facets to his life and his personal being that you don't hear about in Sunday School. He was a great man and an enlightened being in a human body who came to the world to help ease the pain and suffering of mankind. He tried to help us free our minds....just as the Buddha did when he came to the world 2,500 years ago. Both Enlightened Beings gave guidelines on how to walk the path of least resistance. And both beings were misquoted when their doctrines were written down.

There are so many different human cultures and many different practices within those cultures. So....which one is right and true and makes you a good person? Christians will say their path is true. Hindus will say their path is true. Muslims believe they are on the path that is true and Buddhists seek enlightenment and won't fight about who is right. So...WHO IS RIGHT?

Most basically...there is no "right" and "wrong". There is no "good" and "bad" person. It's all about what we believe. Each group thinks their religion is the best and everyone else is pathetic and will go to hell. Talk about a big injustice....this is it.

Shower Time for Serena

Now...Back to Wild Animals. Are humans that much different from them?

I learned alot from my wild animal friends in Scottsdale. I learned love and acceptance from the ground squirrels who ran up onto my lap to grab a peanut and gratefulness from the quail and rabbits as they munched on the food I offered to them. The birds loved the peanuts and mac and cheese.

I was in my kitchen one afternoon cutting up veggies. It was a hot summer day and I knew the rabbits would soon make their trek to rest under the huge pine tree that graces the backyard. And..I mean graces. This is the most amazing tree. No person has ever entered my backyard without making a remark about how beautiful this tree is. I feel very blessed that it flourishes in the yard offering shade to all in the hot Arizona summers.

I put out some carrots and lettuce for the rabbits and some other goodies for the birds and sat down to watch them munch. When I heard some rustling in the tree above my head, I looked up to see this huge bird – a hawk. This was a formidable predator – golden brown in color with a speckled chest. I didn't know what to do because I just put out food for the animals. They would soon arrive and the hawk was waiting to swoop down and grab one. I couldn't let that happen.

Of course, I would never hurt the hawk but I wanted to scare it away so the animals were safe. So I got my super soaker hose sprayer and proceeded to encourage the hawk to vacate my pine tree on this hot day in July. But...rather than fly away, the hawk enjoyed the cool water. It started taking a bath in the spray and fluffed up its feathers. I was so surprised and elated and had such a good time with this bird. But I watched it carefully so that I could avoid any mishap with the animals that would soon arrive. One thing I didn't think about was that the animals knew very well the hawk was in the tree. The only one surprised was me.

The hawk stayed for quite some time and I sprayed it a couple of times – each time it took a bath and then fell to sleep on one foot. Very cute and very big. I later heard from a neighbor that this bird is a Harris Hawk and there is a colony in the big eucalyptus tree in the back of my house across the alley.

The next day, I came out to feed the animals in the afternoon and there was the hawk in my tree again. So...I repeated the ritual we began the day before and the hawk behaved the same way...bathing and then falling to sleep. Then it would fly home to the eucalyptus tree across the alley.

On day 3 we repeated the ritual but low and behold, I found out this hawk was a baby because its mother landed in the pine tree near her. She was darker in color and a bit smaller. She scolded her child and took it home with her. The next day the baby hawk came back and I knew we would be friends so I named her Serena. Practically every afternoon she would come (except when her mother grounded her for being in my tree instead of staying home) and I would spray her and then she would fall to sleep on one yellow foot. Then mom would show up and take her home. When she was in my tree, I would lay in the hammock below and talk to her...I'd call her by her name. S _ E_R_E_N_A...very sing songy...and she would just cock her head at me. Every day she moved lower and lower in the tree branches until she placed herself right above where I was relaxing...in the main crook of the tree. There she would get sprinkled and rest. We built an amazing relationship on water and bathing.

One afternoon she didn't come to get her daily bath so I called her....I yelled across the alley for her...calling her name. To my surprise, she flew over to the tree and commenced with her bath ritual. I thought that was the coolest thing...to be able to call a hawk and she came to see you. She was oh so precious to me and we enjoyed each other's company so very much. Even mom became accustomed to her child's new friend although I'm sure she had no idea of why her daughter was hanging out with the likes of me.

Serena never hurt any of the animals in the yard because she was a baby and still being beak fed by her mother. By the end of the summer, she stopped coming for her sprinkles. Serena was fully grown now, had chosen a mate and was moving on with her life. She never asked to get sprinkled again and I would only see her in passing. It was obvious that our time together had come to an end. She was an adult now and would soon have babies of her own. I miss playing with her in the afternoons but I'll always cherish the relationship we built together.

I left the Scottsdale house In May of 2014 and began my search to find the perfect place in the mountains to live. Then in January of 2017 I returned to prepare the house for new renters. One morning a couple days after my return, I walked outside to feed the birds and heard a hawk screech in one of the pine trees across the alley. If you have never heard a hawk screech, you are truly missing something heartwrenching. It's actually a very scary sound and very aggressive. I guess that's why they use it. I called across the alley to the bird in the tree. "S E R E N A!". The hawk answered me so I called again. You can imagine that my neighbors think I'm a little bit cookoo...but I'm fine with that.

All of a sudden the bird flew across the alley to the pine tree in my yard and landed pretty close to me. I kept saying her name and she kept answering me. I thought to myself, why would a wild hawk fly TOWARDS a person. They distance themselves from humans...not fly closer to them. This hawk had to be Serena – that was the only explanation for its behavior. She remembered me after three years of absence. Another hawk flew over to the tree next to Serena. When she saw him she dive bombed him...landing on his head and chasing him away. She then flew to a lower branch and kept talking to me while I continued to call out her name. She stayed for about 5 minutes and then flew away. And...what a beautiful 5 minutes they were.

A couple of days later, Serena waited for me to come out onto the porch for my morning tea. She flew down on the low branches of the pine to visit me and I knew this had to be my friend who loved to be sprinkled with the hose. What a heartwarming welcome home she gave me. The love I felt in my heart for her was indescribable. This being hadn't seen me in 3 years...what are the odds that she would remember me. But she did.

We humans don't realize how our kindness impacts other beings such as animals and birds. They appreciate kindness. We too many times think they are incapable of love and devotion but this is one indication that such a foolish assumption is incorrect. I could feel the love coming from Serena – as much so as from humans who care for me.

About a week later, I walked outside and Serena must have been flying over my house and spotted me. She gave me a screech as she flew over my head and I called back to her. It was almost like she was saying, "Hi Tara....gotta go feed the kids but just wanted to say Hi!" This connection with Serena and some of the other animal friends I'll introduce you to in this book warms my spirit and I hold those connections close to my heart. They are as precious as other relationships - in fact, maybe more precious because they were unexpected. This story about my relationship with a Harris Hawk named Serena shows that animals and birds should not be abused by humans...they have feelings, memories, and they love. They love their families and they love others...even beings outside of their species.

Case in point: Some people would rather die than allow someone to hurt their pets because the connection is so strong that regardless of what species the pet is, it is part of that person's family. Those are the special people who see the beauty of heart to heart connection with animals. Those people who see animals and birds as a nuisance, something to be abused or neglected, or something to take advantage of for their own end shows their human ignorance. I'm sure I don't have to say it, but those people are disgusting and have no business touching or being with any animals. Animals are innocent... Humans are not.

I left Scottsdale again after spending a couple months in my house and then returned a year later - a change of renters again and I was preparing the house for a couple with horses. I was interviewing landscapers so one company sent an estimator to give me a quote on a monthly yard cleanup (everyone in my neighborhood had a "lawn guy" and I thought since I no longer lived in Arizona, I'd better make sure the property was taken care of).

I was discussing the work I had in mind with the landscaper and a hawk flew over us...screeching. I looked up and wondered if it was Serena. The hawk flew by us and circled around, came back and flew over us again....screeching. I called out "Hi Serena!!" She screeched her reply. I knew she was my friend and I kept saying Hi to her. The landscaper looked at me inquisitively. I told him...that's my friend, Serena...she's a

Harris Hawk and I met her when she was just a baby. He turned to me and said, "I've never seen anything like that...that's amazing!" Yes it was...Serena and I love each other and we remember our time together that summer when she was a baby.

I had an experience with another hawk, however, which began a bit sad. The house I rented in Pagosa Springs, Colorado had huge cathedral windows in the front. One day a beautiful hawk flew into one of them with such force, the house shook. When I looked out the window, the poor hawk was laying on its back with its feet up in the air. OMG...I was devastated. But I sent healing to the bird...didn't go outside, however, because those talons can really do damage.

After I sent the bird healing – in about 15 minutes, I noticed she was sitting upright...thank goodness. It took her over 4 hours to recover and I wasn't sure she would at all. I noticed the ravens starting to gather out in the pine tree in front of the house – near the deck where the hawk was sitting. I thought that was strange until I realized they were contemplating taking advantage of an injured hawk. They probably figured they should take her out before she recovered so I had to stand watch over that injured bird - ready to run out to the deck and chase the opportunists away. Although the hawk was recovering nicely, I didn't want to disturb her by sitting out on the desk in her view. She may have tried to fly away before she was fully recovered – leaving her vulnerable again...so I stood watch for hours from the front windows. Finally, she took off and soared through the air. I don't know if I ever saw her again but I know for sure she never flew into the window after that day. Thankfully, she learned her lesson. The whole incident reminded me of Serena and our afternoon bath times. It brought a tear to my eye.

Animals are rarely afraid of me. They have quick reflexes and react to sudden moves in order to stay alive but as far as fearing me...they don't. They seem to know on a basic level that I will not hurt them. Most people will describe me as wrathful and that's interesting because animals see my true nature and feel no threat from me. Why do humans have problems seeing my intention and my true nature while animals see me clearly? Animals and birds operate through instinct so they see through all the camouflage we humans surround ourselves with. Yes...many humans are dazzled by facades and the "fluff" of a person or event and fail to trust their guts. Maybe it has to do with the cognitive capacity of the brain. My first Buddhist Teacher taught that the more intellectual a person is, the more difficult it will be for them to become enlightened. The conceptual mind truly just gets in the way. So, the simpler and less complicated the mindset....the better for walking the spiritual path. I suppose that's the reason I resonate with the animal kingdom...simple mind with no intellect in the way.

THE PROTECTOR

Because animals know my heart and they know I will always protect them, they come to me in times of danger - when they need food or water or are being threatened by a predator. I was working on the back porch (I called it my office) in Scottsdale as I usually did during the day when a dove flew right towards me...went over my head and landed on the back-porch window sill. Usually animals and birds won't fly at you and stay near unless there is a threat. Gazing out at the back yard, I couldn't see anything brewing but I knew that Serena stayed close to me and she (or one of her family) could be near. I continued working and the dove just sat on the porch.

Within 5 minutes I heard Serena's screech and I knew why the dove was afraid. I remembered that a couple minutes before he flew at me, I heard a skirmish in the pine tree but didn't think anything of it since doves fight with each other constantly. Once the dove sought refuge with me, Serena respectfully bowed out and left the tree. On one hand, I wanted to protect the dove...but on the other, my friend was hungry. So I reminded myself to stay neutral...which I failed to do many times in the past. That's difficult since my first intention is to protect. But nature is nature and it's best if we remain neutral and let nature take its course.

The next morning I was again working on the porch and the exact same scenario took place. The dove flew onto the porch with me and Serena complained. I realized that this was Serena's plan...to return to finish what she had started the day before.

The dove was a baby and an easy target. Serena knew the dove was vulnerable and was coming to me for help. So...she wouldn't attack in front of me. I realized then that Serena had her own set of morals and that included not killing the dove in front of me – not because she was afraid of me – but because she respected me for the kindness I showed her as a baby. So it's clear that she was living by a set of societal rules just as we humans do.

What I Learned from Serena: Be Open to Others and the Beauty of Interspecies Sisterhood

Spencer

SPENCER AND THE FAIRIES

During my time in Arizona, I had ground squirrel friends who I found delightful. When I sat on the porch, they ran up my leg to grab a peanut from my hand. They were the cutest little animals I've met. In fact, I learned the art of giving back from them. As I've already shared – I left my back door open and I would see them running into the kitchen and grabbing a peanut from the peanut bowl...and scampering out to their homes to store it. Every once in a while I would find peanuts in my home that were put there by someone other than me. I found them loving, giving and charming and I learned the art of giving back from them.

My friends vary depending on what part of the country I'm in. For example, I have deer friends in Colorado but not in Arizona. I have ground squirrel and rabbit friends in Arizona but not so much in Colorado. But one group of friends I seem to have no matter where I am are those little creatures who are pure magic....hummingbirds. If you've ever held a hummingbird in your hands, you will most certainly agree with me. There is nothing like it. I've been honored with 3 occasions of holding hummingbirds and each one was mystical. Holding a hummer is like nothing you've ever experienced. Their energy is so different from any being you will encounter and holding them is like holding pure fairy energy....it's magical.

That sounds a little unusual...doesn't it? But it's the truth. Hummingbirds have a knowingness - wisdom that is unlike any other...even humans. They vibrate at a higher level, have a body temperature of 107, and understand humans in an uncanny way. I had a hummingbird go behind me and peck at the back of my neck. Not sure what that was all about but it felt like he was telling me to WAKE UP....

When I lived in Colorado I had two hummingbirds get caught inside my house....remember...it's my habit to leave my back door open! It's difficult to get them out when you have cathedral ceilings. The first one just flew toward the window and kept hovering. When I approached him, he just sat down on the window sill and I scooped him up in my hands...what an amazing experience. His little bill was sticking out between my fingers. I truly was enamored by the little guy and I thought about keeping him inside the house with me. In the end, however, I knew he deserved to be free and I opened my hands and he gratefully flew back to his family.

When the second hummer got stuck in my house, it was soooo difficult to catch him. He kept going up to the second floor and he ran me around that house for many hours until he got so exhausted that he let his guard down and I captured him with a towel by throwing it over top of him. Once again...I was tempted to keep him as a companion but once again I set him free. Since I was a little girl, I dreamed of having a pet hummingbird. But...with age comes wisdom. In my opinion, no one has the right to control another's life so once again, I happily set him free.

I had many hummingbird friends in Scottsdale who came for nectar and I enjoyed being with them immensely. No matter where I live or what group of beings I encounter, I always find one who is extra special and is open to having a close connection to me. Spencer was my close fairy friend. He was a mature, absolutely beautiful male hummingbird. He would sing to me from the pine tree in the morning when I came out to sit on the porch and drink my tea. One day I decided to sing back and from that day on, we communicated in this way. He especially liked to sing in the morning so as I drank my tea, we sang back and forth to one another for 15 minutes or so and we both enjoyed it. He was truly an amazing being and we had a strong connection. He even seemed to understand when I was sad or when I needed some loving care. During those times, he would rarely leave my side for long. He would fly to the nectar and back to the agave plant which stood next to my chair on the porch. As you may have deduced...I would sit on my back porch for hours every day. It was my sanctuary with lush greenery and amazing animal and bird friends.

Hummingbirds may have small bodies but they have the courage of a lion. I have seen Spencer and his family fly around a hawk's face - aggravating him until he gets fed up with that nonsense and flies away. They buzzed around Serena's head a couple of times and watching that just caused my heart to sink. She snapped at them more than once and I kept praying that all my friends would remain safe.

Spencer not only trusted me completely but he also trusted me with his family. I saw that he was courting a female and spending less time with me and then later in the summer I saw baby humming birds all over the back yard. They would zip past me so fast that I only saw wings and a streak of fairydust. I know that Spencer kept them here in the back yard because he knew they would be safe. That was his vote of confidence for our relationship and I loved him with all my heart for his trust.

Spencer taught me the joy of being in the moment. When he sang to me, my heart filled with happiness. He didn't ask for anything...although he did enjoy a big gulp of nectar that I offered him but he asked nothing other than for my love and attention. I will never forget Spencer...ever. He was physically there for me when no one else was and he had a magical way of healing my heart.

When I decided to leave Scottsdale and find a place in the mountains to settle, I was gone for almost 2 years and returned for about a year. My first night in the house, I sat out on the porch as was my habit when I had the honor of being friends with Spencer. Within about 15 minutes, I noticed there was a hummingbird sitting on the agave plant that Spencer used to make his resting place. It was elevated so he had good visibility of the yard. The bird I was watching started to sing to me...and I wondered if this could really be Spencer. Could he really remember me after all this time like Serena had?

I started singing back and my heart jumped with joy as we sat and sang back and forth to one another as if no time had passed at all. This proved to me that just as humans love and have memories of those we connect with, wild animals and birds do as well. Spencer and I were reunited and it felt so good to have my friend back in my life. I

Spencer and the other fairies taught me about magic and that this life is not always the way it appears. These little beings with the heart of a lion inspired me to look for the magic in all aspects of life - you just have to know where and how to look - and then you will eventually see. Most of all...Spencer taught me joy. Even today, when I have hummingbird fairies around me, I think of Spencer and the wonderful moments we shared and I feel uplifted. He inspires me. If a tiny hummingbird can chase away a huge Harris Hawk who is a hundred times his size, then I am also capable of reaching my goal...no matter how difficult it appears.

What I Learned from Hummingbirds: Loving Kindness, Courage, and Joy. I learned how to open my heart to another species who has a free mind and heart.

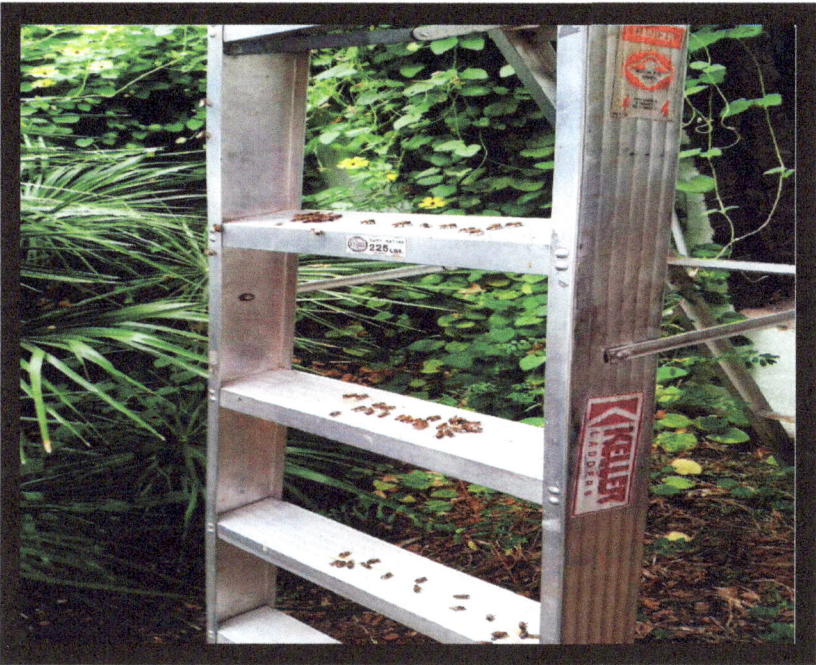

Feeding the Bees

THE AFRICANS - INTERSPECIES COOPERATION

We discussed earlier how our culture and society sculpts our ideas and perception. In essence, they dictate who we are. Perhaps many of you feel this is a bunch of hooey but IT ISN'T. I promise you. Each one of we humans handles an issue or endeavor in basically the same way. Rarely do I encounter someone who truly thinks "outside the box". When I do...I'm so sincerely delighted.

We all know that if we approach someone with disdain or cruelty, he/she won't be open to us or accommodate us willingly. The same is true for our relationships with the animal kingdom...and ultimately our spiritual pursuits. Did you catch what I didn't say? That our spiritual development may possibly depend on our relationship with Nature - with animals, birds, trees, mountains, grass, etc? Well....in a way...it does...but that's for a later chapter. Stay tuned.

I will state it again (and...I will continue to say it): Our culture and society sculpts our ideas and perception. Think about it. From the time we exit the womb until now, we are molded, manipulated and brainwashed by our culture. If we can learn to free our minds and view situations from a fresh perspective, (although not accepted in our society), we can see that a fresh approach may give us a different and rewarding result. And..this will help us see that true altruism can actually transcend realms. It is possible for beings of different realms to respect, trust, and cooperate with one another. This is something I happily experience over and over again as I open my heart to beings from different cultures....and I'm not speaking of beings from the human realm.

A great example of this relates to my honeybee friends. I shared my backyard in Scottsdale with a nest of honeybees nestled in the roof of my back porch. The only previous knowledge I had of bees is from what I read...which wasn't much except that I realized honeybees were quickly becoming an endangered species. I have no issue cohabitating with a colony of honeybees and we lived in harmony for quite some time. In fact, for years. I sensed the nest was quite large but no one ever bothered me and I didn't bother them. In fact, I would never dream of taking the route accepted by most humans - call an exterminator and kill them because I was afraid of being stung. That's a human trait I really detest: A wild being gets in the way...and the action is to hurt them, kill them, etc. to get them out of the way. This train of thought springs from ignorance so for now, we will leave it at that. Regardless....the honeybees and I coexisted peacefully for a long time.

One day I was in the yard refilling the bird bath with fresh water and two bees stung me. One of them stung me in the face which hurt like heck. I thought that was strange because it was so out of the blue. I really didn't think much of it. After all, they must have perceived that I was a threat to their wellbeing or they would have never put their lives on the line to sting. Honeybees die once they have stung so they were definitely committed to their perception of a threat. Then about a week later, I experienced an exact repeat of the earlier incident and got stung again. The attack sent me screaming around the porch and finally into the house...bees chasing me all the way. I ended up in the shower with my clothes on trying to escape the couple that came after me. Luckily I was able to scoop them up from the shower floor, incarcerate them temporarily in a cup and then release them to the great outdoors.

This was a time that I could have gotten very pissed off and retaliated but I realized that honey bees don't sting foolishly. There were a couple of options: I could get stung over and over (which wasn't one of my favorites), I could have an exterminator come and kill them...which wasn't acceptable to me, or I could contact a beekeeper and have the bees peacefully and lovingly relocated. I knew the beekeeper would cost a significant amount of money to relocate the honeybees but that was the only option I could live with.

Any person who is close to me is aware of my "do no harm" philosophy. In fact, my daughter recalls that the only spanking she received as a child was when she and her friend happily and gleefully began stomping on ants that were crisscrossing the pavement where the girls were playing. Ending a being's life is never acceptable to me ....which she found out. Angelique has since grown up to be a gentle, loving, amazing woman – kind to animals, reptiles, insects - to all beings. I must say that she makes me very proud. She told me she will never forget the one spanking she received and agrees that (in hindsight) she deserved it.

Back to the Africans....The beekeeper (John) came and assessed the honeybee nest and told me I had a hive of approximately 60,000 bees living in my porch. WOW. Never saw that comin'. John's idea was to bring a "nuk" – a man-made bee hive for them to live in temporarily while he plugged up the entry to the old hive. And then he would transport the 60,000 bees to his property where he maintained many hives and gathered honey for his family's use. He also placed a funnel on the old nest so the bees could get out of the hive but they couldn't get back in...a one way door so that they didn't get trapped inside the porch eaves and die. As you can probably assume by now...that wouldn't have been acceptable to me. While John was setting up the new hive in his beekeeper suit, the bees attacked him mercilessly. He was shocked at the level of their aggression. They actually chased him down the road after he finished his task. He had to walk up and down the street several times to get them off of his suit.

At that point, John told me he had rarely encountered such vicious bees and that they were deadly Africans. I was shocked because until just recently, they hadn't even paid any attention to me and we lived together in harmony. Considering there were 60,000 opportunities for a sting, I felt that we had a very neighborly relationship carved out. He was so surprised that they hadn't put me in the hospital. He urged me several times to be very careful. "They will kill you, Tara", he warned. Somehow, I knew they wouldn't. The couple stings I received were a warning to me. If I had retaliated, I may not be here today.

I learned a lot about bees from the beekeeper. First, African bees are no more poisonous than Italian or American bees...they are just more aggressive. John explained that when he extracts honey from his bee hives, he rarely puts on a suit since the bees are extremely docile. Once a bee stings you, however, the others react to the pheromones that are released and the rest of the hive comes flying to assist their family. Then you will probably get stung by 15-20 bees. As you probably know, bee stings are extremely dangerous in large numbers. 100 stings can cause organ failure. He also explained that once a hive gets large (as the one at my house), the bees become more aggressive, which explains why I had no issues with being stung until recently. I have to admit, I was unnerved with the warnings.

Every day I witnessed more and more bees taking up residence in the new hive. John had put some honey inside to coax them in and they were happily residing in their new home until one evening I noticed that there were bees covering the nuk. I called John to report that to him and he told me that the hive was full. He came that evening, plugged up the hive and took it to his residence. He told me there would be some stragglers left behind - and that there was really nothing he could do about it but that they would probably die because he was removing their food source and their queen.

That didn't sit well with me so I asked what I could do to keep those left behind from dying. He kiddingly told me I could feed them honey if I wanted to. The visual of me sitting outside feeding bees honey with a spoon made me chuckle but I sat down to formulate a plan. Honeybee queens live a couple of years but worker bees live only 45 days so my plan was to feed the bees for 45 days and let nature take its course. Some would die naturally and some would find another hive to be part of. This experience I was embarking on led to one of the most heart-warming and surprising experiences in my life.

My plan to feed the stragglers was to spread honey out on a cookie sheet and offer it to the bees in the morning and evening. So I spread the honey on the sheet for the bees to eat. This was my first try at feeding African Honeybees and unfortunately, I made the strips of honey too thick. Bees are not very directionally exact when they land...not like birds. Bees are like teetering old planes and so the bees started landing in the wide honey strips and they got stuck in the goo. I started to panic because how can you save a bee who is stuck in honey? I didn't know what to do but time was of the essence so I had to take action. More and more bees were attracted to the honey and soon...all of them would be stuck. Sooo I took the hose and sprayed the bees off of the honey on the cookie sheet and into the grass.

I had a pile of bees in the grass covered with honey and water. I set off to rescue the bees...one at a time - using a small twig and fished each one of them out of the grass and onto the porch table to dry and so they could clean themselves. I was horrified because all I could see was a pile of bees who were not moving and I was so upset because I thought I had done more harm than good. But I was going to do my darndest to save them...one at a time.

As I proceeded with my rescue mission, I soon noticed that bees who had NOT landed on the gooey cookie sheet were flying around the bees that I had just rescued. They would fly down to their family members and nudge them...encouraging them to move and wake up. I've noticed that when bees get wet, (I've fished many bees from the bird bath), they quickly become hypothermic. They just lay there and die. But, if you stimulate them, and get them to move, they will survive. I would constantly fish bees out of the bird bath in the hot summer and then blow gently on them and they responded to the air and started moving. They would eventually clean themselves and fly away.

So this was my method: rescue the bees in the grass, sit them safely on the table or any surface that was warm and safe, stimulate them with air (by gently blowing on them) and hope they survive. And watched as the other bee members flew onto the table and nudged their family members. I witnessed something unbelievable. The unaffected bees and I were working together to save the others in the grass. This was a miracle.

At one point I was leaning over in the yard and trying to find bees that had been doused with honey and water and I realized that some of their family members who were mobile were also flying around and searching for them in the wet grass. When they located a bee in distress, they flew to him. And then I was able to locate the bee and rescue it with a twig – transporting him onto the table to be nudged and nurtured by the mobile bees. The bees and I were actually working together for a search and rescue mission.

How miraculous...that the bees and I were working together to rescue the wet bees. It was quite amazing to me that dangerous African bees and I were working as a team. Until that time, I thought the brain size of a bee was so miniscule that it was impossible for consciousness to exist. But I was wrong. Sooooo wrong. It is true that their brain size is small and they operate mostly from instinct – BUT, somehow they knew I was trying to help their family and we worked together without me ever getting stung.

When we had all the bees out of the yard, the flying bees and I worked together to stimulate the distressed bees - by nudging and blowing air to arouse them. I got some honey for the distressed bees and put small dots of honey around for them to help them recuperate. Bees can look like they are on their last leg...but if you give them a dot of honey, that nourishment will strengthen and revitalize them.

Our rescue effort took several hours but after working together, we saved three-quarters of the distressed bees. And eventually – after they dried out and rested...they flew off. There were about 30 bees that went into the water and 22 came out. Although I felt sad for my mistake, a miraculous relationship that I thought impossible was built.

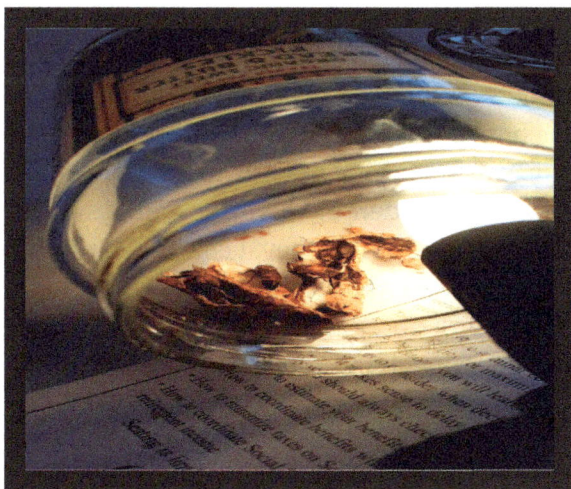

Bee Rejuvenation Device

As I mentioned, bees are extremely vulnerable to hyperthermia. If they get wet and don't have a chance to thoroughly dry out before dark, they cannot fly. If they are earth bound and are stranded out in the open after nightfall...the next day you will find them dead so I created a simple bee rescue device to dry them out quickly so they can fly to their nest for the night. This device was a simple pickle jar with a very low wattage holiday bulb to warm them. I would watch them begin to warm up, then groom themselves (which dried them off), and then exit the jar and fly away.

Later my spiritual guide told me that the bee incident was for a very important reason...to show me that humans and other beings can easily live side by side in peace. We all just need to realize one another's relevance in this experience we call "Life".

Is this utterly amazing...or what? I was so blown away by this experience that I am still in awe of it. It is probably one of the most life-changing experiences of my life. Some of you may not believe this really happened the way it was explained. If I hadn't experienced it myself, I may be a bit skeptical. But, it truly happened and it has changed how I view this world and all the beings who inhabit it.

So...from that point on, I put THIN strips of honey on the cookie sheet every morning and evening to sustain the stragglers of the hive. Once they realized the honey was coming twice a day, they would be not-so-patiently waiting for me to offer them food. They surrounded me as I placed the honey near their old hive and would swoop down like little B-52 bombers coming after the honey. I continued this feeding method until the bees were gone - either to another hive or had died naturally. None of them ever stung me again after we worked together to save lives and I will never forget my loving cooperation with a hive of African Killer Bees.

One of the few people I told this story to was my mom....Mrs. Miriam Kelly. She's someone who took in what I shared with her and truly saw the miracle in it. My excitement wasn't lost on her. She encouraged me greatly because she realized these were stories that must be told. She once shared with me that I'm like no other person she has ever known and that I have a gift to be able to connect and communicate with the animal kingdom and with nature in general. She told me that I have a unique gift that I should share with the world so that others can begin to understand how amazing the animal kingdom is. Maybe someday human beings will truly embrace the beings of other realms and learn to communicate and cooperate with them. At the very least, my hope in sharing this experience is so we can learn to be kind to animals and not harm or kill them. And...Not Eat Them.

What I Learned from the Bees: Interspecies Cooperation

Power in numbers is not always of benefit because bravery without awareness will get you killed...or worse. Yes...there are worse things to happen to us besides getting killed. Having our spiritual development hindered is worse. Trust me...way worse.

I learned a great lesson that when one has a pure heart, it is perceived by others - even those of other species. True cooperation just happens naturally when we work for a common goal - to save other beings.

This experience has changed me forever....

My Home Office (The BackYard in Scottsdale)

ARE WE ALONE? OF COURSE WE ARE

It's New Year's Day and I'm sitting out on my back porch watching the birds playing in the bird bath and eating the peanuts and pancakes I offered them. It's a very peaceful day. I ask myself why I am so happy sitting here alone for the holidays. I then realize that I'm far from being alone. There are so many little beings coming into my line of sight and playing peacefully in the backyard. It's so entertaining to watch them and be part of the festivities.

Most people are with their families or on an extravagant vacation in Telluride or Mexico. But not me. I'm in my backyard. I was invited to spend Christmas with friends but I truly didn't want to be around humans and I asked myself....Why? For a long time, I've been a bit of a hermit and I feel festivities are overrated. But at this very moment, I realize there's something within me that is percolating and that means I'm on the verge of a realization. So, I decided to just let that notion flow through me and see where it ends up. The grackles are fighting over a piece of pancake and Spencer has spent much of the morning chasing other hummingbirds away from the nectar that hangs on the porch. As I watched him chase off a young male, I wondered if he was just a bully greedily protecting his nectar food source or was he actually protecting me....his friend.

I've watched Spencer bravely aggravating the Harris Hawks (including Serena) to keep them out of the yard. He would buzz around their faces and irritate the heck out of them until they left. Every time I saw that display of bravery, I would just pray that the hawks wouldn't get a lucky bite of him. Fortunately his speed and agility served him well in his pursuit to drive a predator about a 100 times his size out of the yard. So I guess I have another defender and there are lots of those honorable beings in this yard. They know this is their home and they defend it with a vengeance. They and I are in this unique learning experience together and it gets interesting at times.

I've been really busy lately building my business and now realize that I haven't spent as much time with my animal friends as usual. I really miss these guys and love them. When one's awareness is covered up by day-to-day responsibilities, we can fail to see the little pleasures in life if we're not careful. I've spent more time outside in the last two days than in quite a while and at this moment, I decide to move my office out onto the porch. Scottsdale is fairly pleasant all year round except for the dead of summer. So the decision was made so I could be near my wild friends and not miss a thing.

Yesterday I had the pleasure to behold Serena and her clan hunting in tandem. What amazing predator birds they are with absolute raw power. And now, I'm watching all kinds of birds playing, fighting and, in general, interacting in their community. I'm one of them.

I finally realize why I'm interested in spending time with animal friends on the holiday. First... I am with the most sincere, real, and loving beings I could ever be with on a holiday. They are pure of heart and take me as I am. With them, there's no reason to do my hair or take a shower. But truly, I ask myself again why I choose to be solitary in the human world and it comes to me. I realize that in the past, I bought into the propaganda that we are not alone...that we have friends and family who have our backs. When the "you-know-what" hits the fan....will that be true? That question is to be investigated today.

In the animal kingdom, mothers defend their babies ferociously but when it comes down to the life of the baby or the mother, usually the mother chooses her life over that of her child. Most times we choose our own safety over that of others. We humans tend to shy away from these types of discussions because we want others to see us as a "good person" or a "great parent". We want to be seen as a person who possesses great courage and compassion who would die in the place of someone we love. But maybe we should take a moment to really embrace this question just to see the reality. I believe we all have a protective nature for those we love and most parents would say that they would give their lives up for their children....but when it really came down to it...would they?

I remember when I was living on the mountain in Colorado and the bear came bounding down the hill towards my cat, Sunny. I ran out into the yard to scoop him up in my arms so the bear couldn't harm him. But what if the bear hadn't turned around and run away? What if he attacked Sunny and me? Would I have given my life to protect Sunny? I don't really know for sure and none of us do because our survival instinct is extremely strong - probably the most powerful instinct we possess.

I ask myself why I am contemplating this aspect of my being and I'm not quite sure of the answer. But I am aware of our sense of "individualism" at all times. In other words, we believe that we have support and back up from family and friends but it is my humble belief that we are always alone because every one of us has a different path. No two people have the same karma or the same experiences. How we see and interact with the rest of the world depends on our culture, how we were raised, our karma, etc. We try hard to support our loved ones but I don't believe we can totally and effectively be there for others in the final analysis.

And so I realized that to be totally clear is to be totally honest with ourselves. We are born alone, we live by our own grace, and we die alone. In between, we enjoy relationships but we should never have the illusion that we are anything other than alone. We can only depend on ourselves and we have to be accountable for our thoughts, actions, words, and deeds. Many times we have the illusion that we have other partners to lean on while we walk our path, but when it comes down to it, we have only ourselves and that is our reality.

I am pretty sure that there have been a lot of gasps out there after reading this last paragraph but realizing that I'm responsible for myself and for my life and am not responsible for anyone else, gives me a sense of freedom. That's the way the animal kingdom operates as well. Every being is in control of his/her own actions and life. I obviously have a peaceful relationship with nature. And some people have told me that I have an uncanny "way" with wild animals. I am not afraid of any of them and we seem to live peacefully together. Those relationships, however, didn't happen by chance. It was a process that took place life after life.

The big buzz word in the human spiritual (and a little in the business) worlds is "transparent". Don't you just love when people repeat things they don't understand? We all know what the word transparent means in English but do we truly know what it means literally or are we just repeating it when the mood hits us or the situation presents itself? If we truly realize what "transparent" means...do we embrace it and make it part of our lives?

Transparency is really difficult for us to experience without leaving us in a very vulnerable position and we wouldn't want to look weak...would we? Transparency truly means that we are open to receiving love and criticism – equally eager to receive both. It's not easy for some of us to receive love – let alone negative feedback. This intense society we exist in has caused many of us to shut down just to survive.

Going into an office and working in a stressful, unhealthy and unhappy environment is painful for spiritual light beings to take. We are, you know, first and foremost spiritual light beings existing in a human, physical condition (as my friend Joe says). I'm not recommending that we should all quit our jobs. But what I'm introducing is the illusion of "permanence". Not one aspect of our physical lives is permanent and any of those things can change at any moment. I speak of this because I've lived through it. I was a corporate employee thinking I was safe and my life was complete. I felt my job would always be there for me because I was a great employee. I was shocked beyond belief when I was laid off and a younger employee was brought in to replace me. I felt like a piece of trash kicked to the curb, felt destroyed and grieved for months. But then I picked myself up and realized that I am much more ....much much more than the job I held. So I started my own business ...and here I am moving my office out onto my back porch.

The pain I experienced after the layoff propelled me forward on the spiritual path. Only when happiness eludes us and we suffer do we seek a way out of our pain. That's why the Buddha Shakymuni sought out the answers to sickness, old age and death.

The Buddha was born into a royal family in India and he lived a life of comfort and bliss until he decided he would like to meet his royal subjects and ventured outside the palace walls. There he witnessed a sick person, someone who was old, and someone who had just died. He never understood the concepts of any of these realities of the human condition before. He returned to the palace and consulted his father. The king, of course, wasn't interested in his son's spiritual questions about old age, sickness and death. The king was only interested in grooming his son to take the throne one day. But Prince Sidhartha was tortured by the continual cycle of birth and death and couldn't bear the thought of his family suffering in this way. He realized he had to find a way to end the continual cycle for the benefit of his family and all living beings.

With a heavy heart, the Prince knew he had to leave his kingdom, his beautiful wife, and infant son to find the answer to the human condition and began living and studying with a group of ascetics who dwelled in the woods, ate only one sesame seed a day and were dependent on no one. Prince Sidhartha could have been considered the first Anarchist. He liberated his mind from the dominion of religion (as well as government controls), he liberated his body from the dominion of property (because he owned only a loincloth), and liberated his being from the government (which was his father). In other words, he removed all constraints from his life in order to find the Truth. He realized that becoming fully enlightened was the only way to end the cyclic suffering of being born, growing old, and dying life after life. He also knew that there was only one way to become enlightened and that was to FREE his MIND.

Freeing the Mind (and Enlightenment) simply means letting go of all the rules and traditions we've been taught our whole lives. Cultural teachings are not the TRUTH...they were just rules made up by a group of our peers. These practices and beliefs are not "right and true". They are just a set of beliefs that were adopted to keep us from chaos. Somewhere along the way these traditions were adopted as the "only way". And that is a huge mistake on all our parts.

You may say, "But Tara, we have to live in this world. So we have to follow the culture's rules". You're right. We have to follow the rules of our country and our culture or we will end up in jail or dead. Although we have to live by certain rules, we don't have to buy into them. As I stated, our culture's rules are merely a result of the decisions of a group of people who put themselves in charge. We can Free our Minds of cultural constraints and still live peacefully with others. We just need to realize from the depths of our beings that most rules are just human-made. Even the religious rules passed down by God, the Buddha and other Spiritual Deities were tampered with and changed by human religious leaders. Now religious rules are used more for control than for the spiritual evolution of the human spirit.

Nature is pure. Nature does not have cultural rules. Trees are just trees and grass is just grass. They grow beautifully all on their own. And my friends....THAT is the reason that I resonate with nature, animals and birds. They live their own truth and are always in the moment because they never know when their lives can end by human hands or by another predator. They are truly transparent. With them, what you see is what you get. So the next time you walk out your back door and see a bird or lizard on your patio, don't just pick up a rake and chase it away because it causes you inconvenience. Your experience with that being could possibly be the greatest teaching of your life. Take my word for it. Appreciate nature and vow to live your life as transparently as nature presents itself. You will be a much happier person.

What I learned from Nature: WE ARE ALONE but that's empowering. We are here on earth to learn how to Free Our Minds so let's be accountable. Not even the Buddha himself can enlighten our mind. That's up to us.

Scottsdale - No Cactus in This Yard!

LEAVING SCOTTSDALE - MEETING MERLIN

I woke up this morning and went about my normal routine – went outside to offer food and water to the birds and animals, sat down to drink some water of my own, and asked myself, "Why am I here? What do I really have to live for?"

Those thoughts kind of shocked me. I didn't feel depressed or sad so I was kind of taken aback. I sat there thinking I want to be here on this earth for my daughter and her family, my Mother and for those close to me so where was this thought coming from?

I was a single woman and our society tries to pair us up. Sometimes people become depressed because they aren't involved in a love relationship and the world around them pressures them to find a mate. I wondered if that was the source of my feelings. Was this an example of our culture messing with my head?

The animal realm doesn't put much importance on a successful 35-year marriage. They just go with the flow and mate with whomever they're attracted to. I have to admit that mating freely holds a lot more promise and sense of reality than setting up a monumental task of keeping a marriage alive for decades. My Grandparents, who had been married for 60 years when my Grandfather died, appeared to have a happy marriage for the most part. However, my Grandmother revealed some wisdom to me during a conversation. She explained, "Your Grandfather and I have been married for a long time so you kinda just roll with it. You're not necessarily happy....you just get into a routine. In my day, you didn't get divorced....that was a No No".

This is a perfect example of our culture changing. When my Grandmother was a young woman, most people didn't get divorced. However, we all know the divorce rate in this country right now....over 50%. So....which practice is "Right"? Is the practice of the old days right and our modern practice wrong? Or is it vice versa? We see on the subject of marriage that the culture has morphed in recent years - just within our lifetimes. This supports my teaching: No culture is right and the other wrong. No religion is right and the other is wrong. One way is not better than the other.

THERE IS NO RIGHT AND WRONG. Instead...there is permanent and impermanent, which is a Buddhist teaching. Permanent things do not change - not ever. Impermanent things change. The only thing that is permanent is the Pure Mind - the Buddha Nature - the Enlightened Mind. It never changes or fluctuates. It just IS. It's like a vast database which holds wisdom and energy. No judgment and no opinion. Everything else is impermanent and will change. Our culture and our religions set the rules for impermanent things. That is why I am writing this book and you are reading it. Our attempts to follow the rules in our culture are creating unrealistic and unnatural expectations for us regarding our behavior. We are no longer living by our innate nature as the animals do. We are restrained by the conscious mind that has been built by living in and abiding by the rules of our society. And this mind is constantly fluctuating and changing. One day we love someone and the next day we don't. One day we want to have a certain career and the next day we don't. One day we want to be married to a wonderful man and the next day we think he's a jerk. The list goes on and on....and on.

I discussed this with a friend one time and she was annoyed by my position....so much so that she stomped away. She told me that I was ridiculous and that I might as well just live with the animals. See how unenlightened her mind was at that point? She thought the human mind was superior to the animal mind. If you put importance on the conceptual mind, then the human mind is far superior to that of animals. Look at technology and all the wondrous "things" we all possess in our homes, cars, etc. But that technology is just a distraction from freeing our minds. Focusing on our job, rushing the kids to school in the morning, taking them to extra-curricular activities night and day, and attending social functions and entertainment with our spouses is just a distraction. Our society places great importance on these things but from a point of view of enlightenment, they are all just a distraction from our primary goal - Freeing our Mind and walking the Path to Enlightenment.

As I again contemplated my strange question - "Why am I here now?" I realized it was simply a question of my reality and perfectly understandable. I wasn't longing for a mate or unhappy with my life. I was just questioning my next step. What did I want to do with the rest of my life? My spiritual progression was my most important aspect and I realized my life was about to change.

I didn't know where my livelihood would come from now that I wasn't working in the corporate world. I had no partner to support me and the love I lost was out of the picture. Maybe these things triggered all the feelings I had that morning but then my Spiritual Guide came to me.

Now, if your eyebrows are raised because I used the term "Spiritual Guide", please bear with me...I'm not losing my mind. We ALL have Spiritual Guides to assist us through our lives. If we didn't, can you imagine what a mess of things we humans would be capable of? We do have guides. Some of us are aware of them and others aren't. I don't see it any different than praying to God or another higher being. It's just a different form.

My Spiritual Guide came to me and told me "Tara – you are asking about the next step because you just want to do what you came to this life to do and somehow you think you're not doing it. You ARE doing it every day – being with animals and birds and living quietly and respectfully in nature. You learn from them and love them all and are helping them as much as they help you. Animals are the only species that humans can share this world with. You humans should all befriend them instead of torturing and killing them. You can help other people see this. I watch you interact with your animal friends so you do your job every day."

I heard what she said but it didn't really settle in for a while. Finally, I realized what the problem was. I had expectations...expectations of what I wanted in this life. THAT was the thing that was causing me pain. I had a vision of what I wanted my life to be, and right now, my life wasn't in alignment with that vision. But the question was, "If I had the life I envisioned, would it really be what was best for me and the work I was doing? AND...was my desire for a life I thought I wanted merely a reflection of the culture's vision of happiness. When I realized how much I had allowed my culture to brainwash me, I was floored!

Of course...our culture teaches us that in order to be "good" we need to behave in a certain way. Otherwise, we are "bad." In order to be "happy", we have to be married and have children. What a bunch of hooey. Many couples are unhappy or they just ignore one another altogether and focus on their work and children. And...why aren't people happy in their relationships? Because they had the same delusion as I did...the vision of what we are taught will bring us happiness. Once again a culture is not "right" or "wrong". There are many cultures that contradict one another in their beliefs and cultures whose customs may be repulsive to us in this one. The important thing to realize is that every culture is simply a group of people who, in order to live harmoniously together, set up a certain set of rules to live by. Some rules are set to keep the peace and others have been set by major religious groups.

And remember who set up the rules - humans -not higher beings. Higher beings like Buddha, God and Allah do not make rules. The Enlightened Mind has no necessity for the likes of rules. My belief is that humans took the guidelines compassionately given to us by higher beings and adapted them to control the masses. And...from the time we entered this world, we have been bombarded by "good and bad", "right and wrong", "yes and no", and on and on. Do you believe I am bashing religion? Absolutely not. I'm just giving my opinion that what Allah, the Buddha and Jesus Christ taught was similar in nature, was changed by the society, and was used to keep this world from supposed chaos. But...have these constraints on our people helped to keep order? I think not. Look at this world and the atrocities that are taking place. If you listen to the news, you will hear one horrible story after another which takes place every day of our lives. None of them will uplift your spirit. Better not to listen...I don't.

The point I am making in this chapter is no matter how pleasant or unpleasant our lives are...remember that this life is temporary and it will change. The one constant in this life is that all things change... so don't get too upset by the "bad" times and don't get too comfortable in the "good" times because the hills and valleys of life will pull the rug out from under your comfort when you least expect it.

My next point of the chapter is that we are all here for a reason. Either we are here to work out our "stuff" or we are here to help others. I've heard people say, "I don't belong here anymore,....I want out." I tell them not to be foolish...THEY CERTAINLY DO BELONG HERE" because their karma drew them here. Karma or destiny (or whatever you want to call it) is the energy that draws us to a certain rebirth and a certain realm of existence according to the state of our mind at the time of death. Buddhists call this concept Collective Karma. Our karmic repository (called the Eighth Consciousness) carries the karmic charges that will pull us into the realm we are most attracted to. Karma is exactly right. We all have our own individual karma and we share collective karma with the realm we are born into. It's a simple "like attracts like" situation. So....the only way we will know that a person doesn't belong here any longer is when they pass on. They leave this life and go to the next incarnation. The next time a loved one dies, allow this wisdom to comfort you. Remember this aspect of karmic accountability and allow it to ease your pain...just a bit.

If you ever feel you don't belong in the life you're in, step back and take accountability for your situation. You...and only you have created it. The good news is that You and only You can change it.

So...back to my thoughts of leaving Scottsdale....

In alignment with what I just summarized about collective karma, was it possible that my life here in Scottsdale was over and it was time for me to move to a new life elsewhere? We don't necessarily have to physically die in order to start a new life. The need for change also drives us into a new living situation - with a new location and new people (and other beings).

I had already lived in Scottsdale for over 20 years - first to accompany and serve my Buddhist Teacher and then just because the habit of living there was easier than moving to a new place and learning to navigate a new life. I was working for a healthcare company in Scottsdale and had an amazing job (because of the salary only) but...I just couldn't withstand the hustle and bustle of the city any longer. I wanted to live out in nature so I could breathe and enjoy the mountains and the wild animals. So I decided to rent out my house, put my belongings into storage and just start driving. It was late May so I would have the whole summer to find the right place. Although I realized my Spirit Guide would direct me, I was also intent on doing my due diligence...that's just who I am.

The packing, putting my belongings in storage, renting the house out to strangers, etc. were all exhausting but the hardest part of leaving Scottsdale was leaving my wildlife friends. I would miss Spencer and Serena so much. I didn't really see Serena every day - she had a family and her own life now. But Spencer and I were together every day... much of the day. I couldn't imagine my life without this little being who made me laugh when I was sad, comforted me when no one else was there for me, and uplifted my spirit with his oh-so-cute antics. I thought I could capture him and take him with me...but in the end...this was his home and his family was here. Although my heart was breaking at the thought of being without him, I couldn't take him with me and I also couldn't stay in Scottsdale any longer.

A week later, I hired a company to move my belongings into storage and met an amazing man - Merlin. I experienced a full array of emotions after meeting him. At first, he annoyed me with his arrogance. But when I watched him wrapping my 5-foot statue of Kwan Yin Bodhisattva with such care, my heart melted. His meticulous care in wrapping and protecting her was so beautiful. He was interesting and after we began talking while we worked, we really hit it off.

He was quite a bit younger than me and because of that, I had no intention of pursuing a romantic relationship with him. I even told him that I wish he could have met my daughter...I thought she would like him. When the move was complete, he turned to me and said, "Do you want to keep in touch with me?" I said to him, "You are too young for me. And in addition to that...I am too old for you." He didn't take No for an answer and asked again...so to be polite, I told him, "Yes...I want to keep in touch with you." I didn't want to upset him but the main reason I needed to stay in contact with him was that he had my bed. My bed (which was so so so comfortable) wouldn't fit into the storage unit I leased. All my other belongings were packed tightly but the bed was sitting there all by itself - alone in the world (hee hee). It was Sunday and the storage facility was closed so I couldn't lease another space. I was in a jam and Merlin offered me a solution. He said he would take the bed back to his house and store it for me until I was able to lease an additional unit for it to be stored. The next day I left for Pennsylvania to visit my Mom and Daughter. It was Mother's Day and that was my annual pilgrimage to the place where my life began....Harrisburg, Pennsylvania - Amish country. So I was very grateful for Merlin's offer....not really knowing if I would see my bed again or not.

When I returned to Scottsdale, I packed my car and met Merlin at the storage facility. He helped me move the bed I had left in his care into a small storage unit and I thanked him for his generosity. He again asked me to stay in touch - that in addition to local moving, he also drove a truck for his company's long-distance moves and he may pass through the general vicinity of where I would be living. He said he felt we should talk from time to time but I again told him I was too old for him - 22 years older but he told me that he saw me as intriguing and he liked me so we left it at that. Quite honestly, however, I was wondering what this guy was up to. Did he feel he could sweet-talk an older woman out of some money? I wasn't sure what his angle was but I was excited about leaving Scottsdale and heading out into the unknown. Where was I going? I had never just packed up and left my home before without some friends or family with me. I was a single woman alone on a journey that may not have been the safest venture but I was intent on finding a new home.

Here we Go!! After leaving Merlin, I hopped into my packed-to-the-gills car and headed north toward Flagstaff, Arizona. I only drove about an hour or so when I realized how exhausted I was. All the activity of the day - packing, cleaning the house, and turning over the keys to my new renters had me a bit tuckered out. And....saying goodbye to Serena and Spencer really did me in.

I made my way up toward the mountains of northern Arizona and had just hung up the phone after a conversation with my Mother. In full Mother Mode...she made me promise to stop driving for the night, get a motel room, and rest. She also requested that I call her every night just for a few minutes so that she would know that I was safe and sound. I agreed with her on both requests and so I began to search for motel rooms along the way.

Low and behold, I found out that I picked a really bad weekend to begin this journey. It was graduation week for the schools in northern Arizona so family and friends were flocking into the area to support their graduates and wish them the best. This was good news for the graduates but bad news for me since motel rooms had been booked for weeks and there were none to be had. I decided to press on. My mother would NOT have approved this decision but the options were to keep driving or sleep in my car and I wasn't in the mood to do the latter (at least not at this point in the evening). So I kept driving toward Page, Arizona. Believe it or not...no motels. Well, there was one for $190.00 a night but I wasn't having any of that. Tired and grumpy, I drove for a little longer and then steered my car into a side-of-the-road turnout which was on a back road in the middle of the desert. Planning on just resting for a few minutes, I closed my eyes and pulled a blanket over me.

Suddenly, a sound startled me and I awoke. At first, I was unsure where I was and how long I had slept. Glancing at the clock, I realized my nap turned into a 5-hour sleep. I again heard the sound that woke me up in the first place. Coyotes! I sat up and to my delight, saw a pack of about 7 coyotes circling my car and howling at the full moon. The night was magical with the alternating full moon hiding and revealing itself from behind the puffy clouds. I was in heaven to be with them and hear their howls. The sound was both comforting and gut-wrenching. So emotional. So primal. So Mother Nature.

After admiring my new friends and watching them until they moved on, I realized it was nearly dawn so I was rested, fresh and ready to continue my journey. I drove through the desert for hours and saw so many beautiful settings in the morning light. But ...surprising to me...all I could think of was Merlin.

I stopped and had breakfast but all I could think of was Merlin. I continued my drive - passing through some canyons that were breathtakingly beautiful but all I could think of was Merlin. All day, he was on my mind and I just couldn't think of anything else. This shows how manipulating the mind can be....doesn't it?

That evening, I found a motel, grabbed some food, and collapsed onto the bed - so tired and spent. But...you guessed it..thoughts of him just whirled around in my mind and I literally couldn't keep myself from calling him. He answered right away and was delighted to hear from me. I told him the truth when I said, "I've been driving through the desert and have seen some of the most beautiful things I've ever seen in my life....and all I can think about is you. He said he had also been thinking of me and thus...the relationship began.

Most chapters in this book bring me extraordinary pleasure and happiness to write but not this one. This one is painful and sad to me but I'm going to write it anyway because Merlin has been and still is a huge part of my path and one whom I love very much.

It was late June now and I continued my journey. In the past, I had spent time in Utah and I knew that (although beautiful) this state wasn't my destination. So I headed north and went through New Mexico, to Wyoming and Montana (where I found my favorite place in the world - Glacier Lake and National Park.) If you have the opportunity to visit, do yourself a favor and go. The glaciers are shrinking due to global warming so they will soon be extinct. There's nothing quite like dangling your feet in glacier water - it's the most interesting color of blue, is crystal clear and very frigid.

In general, I loved the northwest part of the United States but the winters would be brutal and I wasn't up for 30 degrees below zero. I went into Washington state and Oregon - beautiful...but they weren't quite what I was looking for. I had been on the road for months but to my surprise, I was still excited about my journey and the experiences I enjoyed were wonderful and changed my life.

My Mother was having an exciting time as well. As per our agreement, I called her every night after I got settled into whatever sleeping situation I would have for that evening. She strongly encouraged me to check into a motel and not sleep in my car and I honored that agreement most of the time. I was happy to share my experiences with her - she really enjoyed hearing about my travels and explorations. My daughter, Angelique, also kept tabs on me so I was checking in with them every day. I love and honor both my Mother and Angelique for watching out for me - their love and care was undeniable and I appreciated it so much.

Merlin and I talked almost every day as well - even when he was on a long-distance run for his moving company. Although our conversations were usually over the phone, I treasured those times we had together. One day he phoned me and asked how close I was to Bend, Oregon...and that he would be there that evening. Interestingly enough, I had just left Bend and was only about an hour away so I immediately went back and found a motel suite. I'll never forget how I felt as I waited for his arrival. Excited....a nervous wreck....ready to meet my perfect match.

We had a most magical time together those couple days but the rest of our time together involved anger, dissatisfaction, and pain on both our parts. We came from different worlds and weren't able to really bridge the gap between us and understand one another fully. I didn't see how he and I could ever build a long-term relationship but when we were together, the beautiful energy between us was undeniable. I hadn't really had a man in my life since my divorce in 1990...so there was quite a period of time that I lived solo. I committed to myself that the only way I would ever enter into another relationship was if it was extraordinary.

Energetically, this one WAS extraordinary but on a physical level, we were both dissatisfied - perhaps due to the age gap or perhaps because of the ethnic differences. I realized Merlin would hold a monopoly on my heart whether I was with him or not. Here I had finally found someone who I could be extraordinary with but the differences between us left us both disappointed.

I even traveled back to Phoenix for a month to spend more time with him - to try to solidify our relationship but I believe he was already seeing another woman and the time he spent with me was minimal. I was heartbroken because I had a vision of he and I and a life together....a mountain home where I raised chickens (for eggs not meat), a garden to raise fruits and vegetables...a place of solitude for me – where I would give Dharma class once a week and then live peacefully and happily secluded from the public eye. He would go to work during the day or on overnight runs...and when he came home, we would be elated to be together. This arrangement would give us time together and also much-needed time apart where we could both be free unto ourselves.

When I finally found the area I chose to live in, he promised he would come to spend time with me one long weekend each month and we would "see where our relationship goes". That sounded like a plan to me and even though I didn't speak of it, my plan was to also go back to visit him one weekend a month as well.

He never came....not once. And my heart broke into a million pieces. Finally...I realized it made no sense for me to hold on to him...and I stopped taking his calls. I had to put it behind me and try my best to heal my heart. I had met my perfect match and we were unable to build a relationship and life together...at least for now so it was time to stop torturing Merlin and myself. My spiritual guide comforted me during my darkest times. She explained that I am here in this life to teach the Wisdom of Freeing the Mind so that others can gain perspective on their lives. She also explained that I am walking the path of compassion in her footsteps so she taught me the way so I can share with others.

Would I consider inviting Merlin back into my life? He's told me that he wants a "normal life" with children and someone to be there for him when he comes home from work. I do understand. The normal life he desires is easier....much easier than it would be with me. A life with one's Perfect Match propels one into a huge growth spurt because the two together produce magical results. I shared with him that life with me would be challenging but it would force him to work out his past karma, learn to Free his Mind, and live an extraordinary, magical life. The choice was his and he chose the easy way.

I'm writing these next couple of paragraphs for Merlin - trying to find a way to share some wisdom with him. I hope he gets the message. Merlin lost his magical life a long time ago because of unspeakable treachery he was involved with in another lifetime. Because of that karma, he cannot manifest what he desires so he has great hopes and dreams but no power to bring those hopes and dreams into fruition. He continually chooses to live as a big fish in a small, stagnant pond rather than bringing forth his bravery and having the courage to start out as a small fish in a vast ocean where he has space to grow. I hope he remembers that living as a big fish in a small pond is dangerous because at some point, he will cease to grow. Even worse, some day the small pond may dry up and then where will that leave him?

Merlin...I know that your life is a disappointment to you and has been very painful. However, there's only one way to correct it and you're going in the opposite direction than you need to. There's only one way, my darling, and it lies with resolving your karmic debt and Freeing your Mind. Don't wait too long to resolve this....

PAGOSA SPRINGS

It was October and I had been on the road for over 4 months. Surprisingly, I had adapted to this gypsy-like lifestyle. It was tough to work for a company (9-5) while on the road - especially since they didn't know I left Arizona! There was one time that was particularly challenging. My manager called a spur-of-the-moment team meeting and she planned on traveling from Texas to Scottsdale so she could meet with the staff face to face. WOW...I had to drive all night to get there for the meeting. And...by the time I was half-way to Scottsdale (which was a total of 12 hours), she abruptly cancelled the meeting. Needless to say, she wasn't my favorite person at that point but that's the way the cookie crumbles when you're living a secret life!

After much research and travel and some urging from my friend, Kim, I found a beautiful place to live in Pagosa Springs, Colorado. There it was...much as I had pictured it...a large house to rent - right on the side of the mountain. Such a house was much too big for me alone but with all the promises Merlin was making, I felt that in time, he would consider moving to Pagosa to be with me. As I stated earlier, he had already committed to coming to visit me "one long weekend a month" so I was hopeful that it would work out for us and I laid the groundwork for him to be with me by investing in this place where there was plenty of space for both of us. The house even had a mother-in-law apartment beside the garage which would provide some private space separate from the main house.

The house would be ready for me to move in on November 1 and it was now the beginning of October so I rented a kitchenette in a cute motel on a creek within the town limits. It was the size of an efficiency apartment and I was quite comfortable. The main thing was that it had a kitchen, refrigerator and stove. I have dietary restrictions and am a vegetarian so I usually cook my own meals. That way I know the ingredients are organic and have no allergens.

My Mother always told me that I'm not happy unless I have wild animals around me to make friends with and she's right. So, here in this motel kitchenette in a beautiful place, on the creek where the deer look in the windows in the morning, I found my next wild friends....ground squirrels. They were beyond cute and mischievous as can be. One day I threw one of them a peanut. The next day...I did the same and soon, they were my new best friends. They had a family of about 7 or 8 and somehow the number kept growing.

The weather was pleasant so I decided to leave my motel door open during the day while I worked which encouraged them to come in and visit me. So I threw peanuts near the door, inside the door, etc. Soon they were running into my hotel room to grab a peanut and scurry out to bury it in their treasure trove of assorted delicacies. My relationship with them brought back fond memories of my ground squirrel friends in Scottsdale.

It was a Saturday morning and I decided to sleep in for a change so I lingered in bed for a little longer than normal. All of a sudden, I heard a scratching sound. Then I heard it again. Soon it was really annoying so I looked up and what did I see? No surprise. Two ground squirrels were clawing at the screen of my window (which was open) telling me to get my lazy butt out of bed and give them some breakfast. I laughed out loud and noted the audacity and the beauty of these animals. They have no constraints binding them such as pride or protocol. They always come from the heart and that's what I admire about them. So, I got up and served breakfast and that's all it took to make those little beings the happiest in the world. As I said before, "Feed them and they will come!"

Soon my month's stay at the Ground Squirrel Motel came to an end and I was ready to move into my new rental home. The move didn't take long since all the belongings I had at the moment in Pagosa Springs were in my car so I only had to back it up to the door of the house and a half hour later, I was moved in. It was strange being in this big house with no furniture...but Merlin assured me he would help me move my belongings from the Scottsdale storage area to my new home in Colorado. At that point in time, I was sure that he wanted me in his life and that once he helped me move to this place and spent some time here, that he would love it. And...in time...he would be here with me.

To make a long story shorter, I did everything I could to build the relationship with Merlin. I would drop everything to meet him on the road when he was in Colorado for a long-distance move. Even though we were supposedly together, he never helped me move my belongings from Scottsdale to Colorado as he promised. He kept trying to put me off to a later time - telling me he was "super busy right now". He was "super busy" alright. Super busy with someone else.

I had waited over 2 months for him to keep his promise and wasn't waiting any longer. So I got a ride back to Scottsdale, rented a moving truck and hired moving people to help me on both ends of the trip. I was hurt by Merlin's lack of caring for me but I had to be strong and complete this mission so I hopped in the truck and began the journey from my past to my future. I was starting a new life. The trip was uneventful until the last two hours when it began to snow. Here I was with a truck full of furniture and was fairly inexperienced driving anything bigger than my Hyundai. Throughout this blizzard all I could think about was the contradicting messages Merlin was giving me. I kept my end of the bargain but Merlin never did. He never kept one promise he made to me. Was he just trying to use me - an older woman whom he thought would do anything for a younger man? I'm not sure what his motive was but his absence during this time, when I really needed him the most, was the final straw! The relationship fell apart.

WHO ARE WE...REALLY?

My first few months in this beautiful setting on the outskirts of Pagosa Springs, CO - on the side of a mountain (my dream location) should have been some of my happiest of times but, instead, they were some of the darkest of my life. It was early morning and the sun was barely peeking over the mountain ridge. These mornings were a magical time for me...time when I experienced realization about my path and my next steps so I treasured them and rarely missed a sunrise. As I sat on the back porch, watching the Stellar Jays diving for the peanuts I offered them, the baby skunks foraging through the compost patch, and hummingbirds chasing one another and fighting over the nectar, I thought back over my life and the choices I had made.

By choice, I didn't marry young. I was 29 when I took the plunge and as I look back, he was definitely the right man for me at the time. We were together for about 8 years and then after my daughter turned 3 years old, we divorced. It wasn't his fault. I was progressing on my path and he wasn't interested in going in that direction so we parted.

After my divorce, I chose not to enter into another emotional entanglement. I dated a few times but there were no serious relationships - none that even came close to materializing. Frankly, I met few men who really caught my eye and those who did weren't really on a similar path that I walked. My destiny was becoming clear to me and I was sure there was no stopping it. Its momentum was like a huge boulder rolling down the mountain. Just try and slow it down! So, I decided to continue my internal work and walk the path I was born to walk. By the time I met Merlin, I had been divorced for almost 25 years and after all that time, watching my relationship with him crumble only added to the pain I was experiencing.

I just wanted to be left alone....and alone I was except for my beautiful wild animal friends. They were plentiful on the mountain. Deer came into my yard as well as skunks, weasels, wild turkeys, hummingbirds, squirrels, foxes, elk, and even cougars. And...I did see wolf tracks on the top of the ridge during a trek even though wildlife organizations stated there are no wolves in Colorado except those in Rocky Mountain State Park which was hours from my house. I guess the wolves didn't realize they weren't supposed to be on the ridge behind my house. I can't imagine that wolves would have the audacity to break the man-made rules regarding my back yard...and someone really should have informed them that they didn't live near my house. Sounds ridiculous, doesn't it. You bet! Just as ridiculous as some of the rules that the human realm has created for itself. We'll discuss more on this later. I absolutely love wolves so I'm thinking that my desire to live with them brought them close to me.

These pleasant thoughts streamed through my consciousness but way too soon I returned to my emotional pain. The loss of a loved one is so tough. It definitely can either throw one into a tailspin and deep depression or it can push those of us on a spiritual quest for the truth into deep contemplation. Fortunately, what happened to me was the latter and nothing short of miraculous. That's when the path became personal for me.

One huge realization I've had as a result of my strong bond to nature is that when you take a being...no matter who they are...and strip everything away...there they are. That's when they are "real."

Have you ever wondered why everyone likes trees? Who doesn't like a tree? You have to work really hard not to like them...they are beautiful and flowing and take great pleasure in shielding us from the sun and elements. They are romantic and bring about great contentment. We sleep under them and rest to meditate with our backs against their trunks. We all understand trees expel oxygen which we require to live but...the response we humans have for trees is not that of need...it's emotional. Why? Because they are non-assuming, asking for nothing from us, and giving freely to those who live among them. In other words, they are "REAL".

It's the same for wild animals and birds. A couple years ago I was traveling through Idaho (one of my favorite places because of its wilderness) and I saw people pulling their cars over to the side of the road. I tend to be curious (or maybe nosey) so I stopped and rolled down my car window and asked what they were looking at. A woman whispered to me that there was a bear in the clearing and they all were hoping it would come closer so they could get a better look. I chuckled. First of all, that bear ain't coming closer to people gawking at him/her. And second, it struck me so funny that when people are on vacation, they're interested in wildlife but let that bear trek into the home's backyard and they will be calling the fish and game commission to come and use whatever force necessary to remove that bear from their neighborhood.

Animals and birds are real and, in general, many humans tend to be fickle and self-serving. Any animal, bird, insect or reptile that inconveniences us is a nuisance so we want it gone and we don't really care in what form that takes place. Why do we see that our human lives are so much more precious that those of the animal realm? We humans have literally made many of the animal realm our food source, our beasts of burden and our whipping boys. The only exception is our pets whom we cherish and would fight to death to protect.

So why are our pets more important than other members of the animal kingdom? You know the answer to that question. Because they belong to US. They provide emotional support to US. We as a species are many times exceptionally self-centered, self serving, and totally disregarding those who serve no purpose to US. My statement sounds really severe doesn't it? Yep...that's because it is and we need to change that in order to live peacefully in this world with others. I guarantee you that every being in this world considers his/her life just as precious as we do ours. We humans would be better off if we realized that.

From my perspective, the definition of love is that it is unconditional - with no restraints or limitations. So, are we really unconditional with our pets? Human nature is bound by stipulations and "if-then-else" scenarios. Would our pets love us if we didn't offer them food? Would we love our pets so much if they refused to show us love and affection...or even worse, showed us aggression? If those two things changed the nature of our relationship with our pets, where did that love go?

Many of us have gotten married and promised to love our spouses forever. But more than half of those "forever" relationships fail and end in divorce. Even worse, many of us stay together for convenience. Where did that love go? Too many times we make a promise and break it and that makes us bad people right? WRONG!

Religious and Spiritual groups teach that love and compassion are the answer to a peaceful life - especially in these times where it seems that not even a week goes by without some sort of tragedy. "All You Need is Love", "Put a Little Love in Your Heart", "Love One Another as I Have

Loved You" Is love really the answer? In my opinion...it certainly doesn't hurt. It would be so great to heal our relationships with one another even though there are huge differences between races, sexes, religions, and cultures. Why can't we just let others be themselves and we mind our own business? Because we need to control our world or we feel too vulnerable....too exposed. We depend on our rules of society to hold us upright and to give us something to lean on. Some day we humans will heal our hearts and be able to live happily with diversity but, for now - to start our healing process, there is an easier, less intimidating place to start - The animal kingdom.

Wild animals want nothing from us except safety. Their lives are very precious to them - just as our lives are precious to us. They will enjoy a morsel of food if we choose to give it to them but those creatures are free, self-sufficient, and they have everything they need. They don't need us but they are curious about us. I have spent a lot of time with wild beings and one thing I have learned is that it requires the utmost patience. It takes a bit of time for them to trust us. Their curiosity about us will help form the relationship but patience is the key. Contrary to relationships between humans, you always know where you stand with animals. They don't pull any punches. When gentleness, acceptance and calm-abiding is added to the mix (along with patience) magic can take place. And...I mean magic.

Although creating a relationship with a wild animal takes a lot of patience, it is so much easier than bonding with humans. The relationship is created on an innate level so there is no pretense. It can be a challenge, however, because you have to come from a pure place in your heart to build a relationship with someone who doesn't want anything from you. It's pure...it's real...it's nature. So, maybe this is a good place to start to realize who we are and to build a relationship with those who have no agenda.

I created my first chapter of Free the Mind (a way of releasing karmic entanglements from one's mind - to lighten the mind) with the help of my animal friends. I watched how the African bee colony interacted and cared for one another in Scottsdale. I watched as my wildcat friend, Sunny, laid down boundaries but lived peacefully with the skunks who resided under the barn in Pagosa. I watched as Spencer annoyed Serena by buzzing her head to get her to leave his domain. And I watched as she tolerated him because she knew he was one of my closest friends. I witnessed how they lived their lives purely and that raw beauty melted and healed my heart.

When we make friends with wild animals we should be careful not to try to make them our pets....they won't allow it. They appreciate a morsel of food or a drink of water but they will never allow us to control them. They are free and they intend to stay that way unless force is used. We humans could learn this important lesson from our animal brothers and sisters: "Never compromise your freedom. Never let them take away your right to orchestrate your own life. Never let them render you as a slave." It's clear to me that we human beings are stuck in a society of countless rules and regulations - and we have given up our most precious rights. Wild animal friends haven't...so who is in a place to teach who?

We humans are superior intellectually because of our ability to reason, conceptualize and create. BUT...our animal brothers and sisters are far ahead of us on the path to Freeing the Mind. They don't have to bypass their intellectual minds to investigate who they are as we do. They don't have to work for a living and participate in a modern society that places more importance on making money, "living the dream", and searching for happiness than making spiritual progress. They don't have all the worries and constraints that humans do. So.... which realm is superior? It all depends on one's path. If our desire is to become CEO of a billion dollar corporate firm, we should stick to the ways of the human. But...if we are interested in enlightening our minds, walking the spiritual path, and helping others to do the same, we would be wise to follow the model of the animal realm rather than the path we're already walking.

This may sound strange but building a relationship with a wild animal or bird may feel like it puts us in a vulnerable position. When Spencer came onto the porch to partake of some tasty nectar, I didn't pay much attention at first. There were many hummingbirds who came to eat but I started noticing that this guy was different. I think he was curious about me....this person who would sit on the porch for hours. I soon started to realize he wanted to understand me and somehow he knew my heart was broken. I didn't know how to nurture my own heart and his heart was totally open. There was no facade. Spencer showed me exactly who he was. He was an open book and that scared me at first. I was ashamed that I was not as open as he was. I looked at myself over and over again and realized that the way we humans interact with one another is so different from the way Spencer and I bonded.

When you encounter a tree, animal, bird or any part of nature, you behold beings in their naked state. Nothing is hidden - it is what it is. You see exactly what is there with no spice or sugar on top. It's uncomfortable at first because we humans are used to living with a shroud over us – rarely showing others too much for fear that they will not like us. We are used to living behind our ego which covers up our burdens, our pain and our misgivings. However, when we behold nature, it shows us all its attributes - at first glance. So...when we are brave enough to put aside our fear, we will see the absolute awe in finally beginning to experience the truth. And...if we are brave enough to remain on that path of self-discovery and follow our innate compass for our higher good, we WILL walk the spiritual path to enlightenment. And then...I hope we will remember those who helped us along the way - our animal kingdom friends so that we will never again use them for food, beasts of burden, or any other demeaning purpose. Nature and our animal realm friends can and will help us turn our lives around if we are patient with them and give them a chance.

So...right now we are NOT living as our true selves. Why? Because that would make us too vulnerable in this cruel world, wouldn't it? Would we get hurt if we show who we really are? Maybe. But so what. When someone is rude to us or disregards our feelings, which part of us is hurt? Is it our True Nature? Or is it our ego mind? You know the answer to that one.

You may challenge me and say, "Tara...when I open myself up to those I love, they break my heart." Truly I ask, "Do they really break your heart?" What did your loved ones do to break your heart? What part of your heart did they break? Did they actually do harm to your physical heart? No. Actually, what is hurt is the ego. The ego wants, expects and demands. Sometimes people can't or won't give us what we want so we feel "unloved." Sometimes people don't meet our expectations so we suffer. Did they break our hearts? No...they just couldn't or wouldn't meet the demands of the entity who holds us hostage - the big E. We privately ask ourselves, "How dare they not give us what we want when we are so great?" All of this is ego - not the Pure MInd. The Pure Mind wants nothing and needs nothing. It is complete just the way it is. This pure part of us isn't good or evil...black or white...best or worst. IT JUST IS. Do we really make ourselves more vulnerable by being our true selves rather than trying to appear better to the world? Or does that love and acceptance of our True Nature and the realization of who we really are make us stronger? If people don't like us....Tough! We didn't come to this life to please others. We came to walk our spiritual path. On this path, we walk alone so please be true to yourself.

I vowed a long time ago that I would be myself no matter what. Sometimes those around me accept what I teach and sometimes they think I'm nuts. So what! If someone doesn't accept me as I am, then they aren't worth having as a friend.

So who are we...really?

Let's start the process by discovering who we ARE NOT. Are we the body? Are we the mind? Are we our emotions....our intellect, or our accomplishments & failures? When we meet other people, we shake hands and say, "Hello...I'm Tara". If you think we are the body, which part of it are we? If we are the body, then we can't be the mind...right? And if we are the mind, then we can't be the spiritual self so who are we?

We are not the body – That's Impermanent.

We are not the ego mind – That's Impermanent.

We ARE the Spiritual Essence – That's Permanent.

You will rarely hear me talk about the "Truth" because there are very few truths in this world and there are mostly opinions and perceptions when speaking about our lives. The only part of us that is the "Truth" and is permanent is our spiritual nature. When we die, the body and all our emotional hang ups – likes and dislikes – everything related to our physical being, will be discarded. How often do we think of ourselves as spiritual beings...when we are at church or temple? Or when we are reading a spiritual book or meditating?

Most times we ignore the pure part of who we are...the only real and permanent part of our being. I'll repeat this because it is extremely important – **The True Nature is the only part of us that is real.** The rest of us (and that is a huge part) is just fluff. Specifically, the impermanent part of us is simply the ego spinning a web of concealment to show the world only what the ego wants it to see about us.

How can we identify what the real part of us is? It's the part that doesn't change. How many things can we identify in the physical world that never change? The body changes...the mind changes and the ego certainly changes every step of the way. Everything that is organic is born, grows old, and dies. Concrete is very strong but eventually, it disintegrates. Even Mountains erode and break down over time. So...everything we perceive with the 5 senses and the mind sense is changeable and, therefore, not real.

Does it blow your mind to realize that everything we see, hear, touch, smell, taste, and think about in this world is NOT REAL? When my first

Buddhist Teacher said those words, I thought my mind would explode. If the data we bring in from the senses is impermanent and isn't real, how do we orchestrate our lives? Further, how do we live this life without feeling the ground will continue to crumble under our feet? What do we lean on now that we realize this truth? It's a frightening realization at first but we just need to shift our view....just a little bit.

Only when we begin to witness the real part of us (the Pure Mind) will we truly be at peace. It's best not to talk about happiness as a goal because think about it....what part of us would want happiness? You guessed it – the protector of the physical...the Ego. Have you heard people talk about their families saying their children or lovers make them very happy? That's fine as long as they realize that emotional matters are temporary...they are impermanent. Need we talk about the divorce rate in this country to lend evidence to my statement? Our society drills into us that our goal in life is happiness. But happiness is a human desire that is fleeting and fickle. Our animal siblings don't seek happiness – they seek to stay alive. Having a calm and peaceful mind (and freeing the mind of its karmic burden) is the path that leads us to our enlightened state.

I've heard teachings and read books that proposed that the only way to progress on the spiritual path is to assert oneself and nurture self esteem by not allowing others to have control over us. That's ridiculous! I don't propose that we allow others to take advantage of us in any way. However, it's best to see things as they are. These matters of embellishing self esteem are ego driven...the True Nature couldn't care less about any physical-world phenomena. It takes no interest in the pursuit of our wildest dreams, making millions of dollars, finding the cure for a disease, or winning the Nobel Prize. The physical world was manifested so beings can resolve their karma. With that in mind, would it make sense that it is advantageous for us to stop creating karma so we don't have to resolve it? Let's stop the bleeding first – by realizing how and why karma is created.

I do not propose that we avoid connections with other humans and others of different species – I'm just suggesting that we may want to rein in our expectations regarding other beings because they have their own spiritual path to walk...just like we do. Sometimes we meet spiritual friends who remain in our lives and sometimes they come into our lives for a short time and are gone. This is because everything that is impermanent changes.

We humans pursue relationships as if we believe they will last forever and they rarely do. When these relationships don't work out the way we expect, there is pain and disappointment on the part of one or both people. Most times, there will be emotional entanglements with any relationship because one or both of the parties will literally not get what they want from it. With regard to emotional entanglements, animals have few and they really have no expectations of the future.

I've seen this display with Amos – the deer. You will read more about him a little later in the book. I became friends with Amos when I first moved to Crestone, Colorado. He would wander into my yard every afternoon while I was working in the yard. If I offered him food, he was grateful. If I didn't, he didn't get mad and gore me with his antlers. The next day and the day after that, he would show up as usual to see if there was a snack for him unless he was busy traveling or mating. His life is simple.

Amos and all of my animal friends have a desire to live (or they wouldn't be alive) but beyond the basic instinct to survive, they don't have a lot of desires. They search for food in a place they found it in the past (that is a survival instinct) but if the food isn't there, they take their search elsewhere. There are animals who mate for life but most don't. Most animals have their mating mantra: "If you're not with the one you love...love the one you're with...or love many you are with". Humans are similar to our animal friends physically but that's where the similarities end. As we continue to modernize, we move farther and farther from our True Nature. We are filled with all kinds of desires. We have an expanded need for comfort, good food, recognition, love, adornment, etc. The list

96

is endless. So those beings in the animal kingdom have much simpler minds and, therefore, purer minds than humans. And we humans (for the most part) feel animals are stupid and expendable. So which species has the more enlightened mind? Whose mind is freer? We humans would do well to wise up and see what's truly in front of us instead of what our society teaches us. I am not proposing that we begin to live as animals. I'm proposing that we can learn from animals and use their spiritual model to Free our Minds.

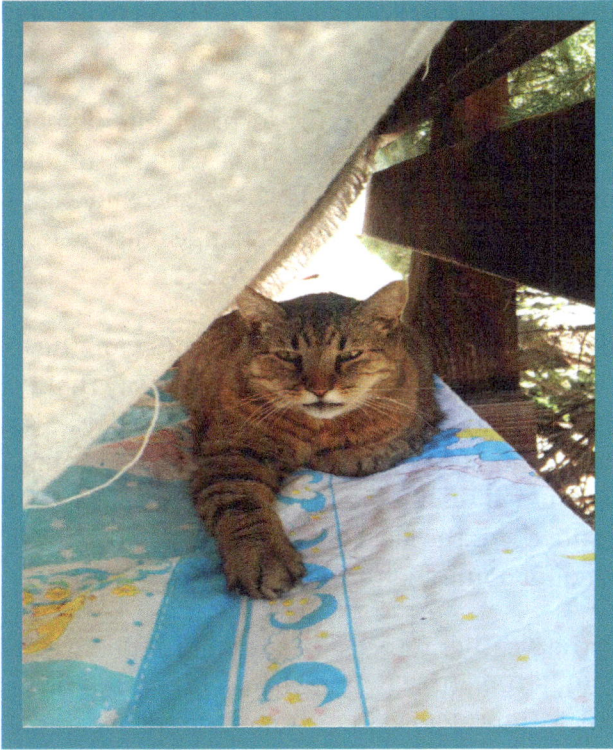

My Comrade - Sunny

SUNNY

It was mid-November and I had only been in the new house a couple of weeks but it was pleasant enough during the day to sit out and relish the mountain's beauty. The pines lined the ridge behind the house and were the main inhabitant of the yard. In fact, the yard wasn't flat - it was angled upward because I was literally located on the side of the ridge. I loved it. I would sit on the back porch in the morning and admire the trees. I love trees - especially pines. I was moved in. Of course, most of my belongings were back in Scottsdale so all I had to unload and put away were the items I had packed in my car.

I never liked cats. They made me sneeze, break out in itchy welts, and ultimately my body created an asthmatic reaction - trouble breathing. Because of my body's sensitivity to cats, I never really set up an alliance with these beings. But that was soon to change one late fall afternoon in Pagosa Springs, Colorado.

From the time I moved in, I had seen a cat running on the top of the ridge. He looked like a bobcat but he was so far away that I couldn't really be sure. He definitely looked wild. Within a couple days, I saw he was making himself at home - laying in the sun outside the barn on my property so I assumed that he was sleeping in the barn at night. We had gotten some snow over the last couple of days so I figured he was hanging around for some shelter and warmth.

After hearing the weather forecast (we were to get between 15 and 20 inches of snow), I thought..."Geez...we haven't gotten rid of the snow we already got earlier. But, I lived in the Colorado mountains at an elevation of 7,000. What did I expect? I chuckled to myself, "Tara, you are no longer in Scottsdale!"

Around 4:00 in the afternoon, I heard a being crying. I looked out and saw this cat sitting on the porch crying his little heart out. I walked out to greet him and met this beautiful gray tabby but there was definitely another breed with long hair intertwined in his family tree. He looked wild and that's what intrigued me. He wouldn't really let me touch him (and I didn't want to because of the allergies) but he wouldn't leave and I had no food for him. I gave him a veggie burger (hee hee) but he wouldn't have any of that. I was a vegetarian who was trying to feed a meat-eating cat with my own food resources...didn't work so well. So I went into town and bought milk and cat food. He drank a little milk and finished the entire can of cat food so I figured he may not have had a successful hunt in a while.

Snow started to gently meander its way down through the evening sky and I felt horrible at the thought of leaving the little guy out in the snow and cold. I thought I would set him up in my mudroom so he wouldn't really be in the main house. There was a half door between the mudroom and the house and he would be warm there with the blankets I laid down for him. However, he decided he wasn't staying in the mudroom. Remember...I never had experience with cats or I would have known how ridiculous it was for me to believe a cat wouldn't hop easily over a half door. I was worried I would get sick if I kept him in the house. So...I took him down into the garage, gathered up the blankets I had already set him up with, grabbed a couple of throw rugs to keep him warm and introduced him to his own condo in my garage - complete with an oil-filled heater, food and water. He had a sweet little set up for the night so I wished him sweet dreams and left him there to enjoy his new home.

The next morning I recapped what had happened the night before: I have a severe allergy to cats but last night I was going to allow a cat to sleep in my mud room. I created a living space for the cat in my garage. I love all animals but I didn't want a pet that I would need to take responsibility for. I loved to behold wild animals and offer them a morsel of food but wasn't interested in taking on this kind of commitment. But, this little being needed my help and I was happy to assist him.

I went to town and got all the necessities for the cat - a bed, toys, food, litter box, etc. I couldn't believe I was doing this but I would never let an animal suffer and he clearly wasn't used to being in the snow. He wouldn't even put a foot into it. For now, this homeless cat was safe, warm and fed and I would care for him until the storm passed.

When the sun came after the storm, all the trees sparkled as the light bounced off their snowy branches. It was so pleasant and much warmer so I decided to release the cat from the garage and put his food and water on the deck. I knew in my heart I had to give him back his freedom and figured that he would eat and take off. Or...he would roam the mountain side and then come back for food once in a while if his hunting effort was less than successful. Or...he may come back when the weather was cold and snowy so that he would have a nice warm condo to sleep in at night. Any of those scenarios was fine with me, although in just a couple days, I had grown fond of the little guy.

Well...the cat had a different idea and didn't accept any of my proposed scenarios. HE NEVER LEFT! I watched as he patrolled the perimeter of the property like a security guard. He would walk all the way to the top of the mountain ridge and then back down the other side and around the house. All that physical exertion produced an appetite so he would then take a few bites of food and stretch out on the porch - in the sun. Each time he left for one of his excursions, I thought I may not see him again but he soon returned as if he had done so for years. He had made his home in my home and found a special place in my heart. The amazing (and very fortuitous) thing was that I didn't have any allergy symptoms when I was near him. That was truly magical. How was that possible? Simple...it was meant to be.

I wondered what I should name this cat who had adopted me. I usually name the animal friends I encounter just so I can call them by a name that they will recognize my voice. Sometimes the names come right away, sometimes in a few days, and sometimes they come after trial and error. For this cat, it was easy. He had a kind of grumpy look on his face much of the time and that was his personality - grumpy, demanding, loving, devoted, and my friend and comrade so I named him Sunny...hoping that the name would lighten up his disposition. Hee Hee.

At that time, I worked remotely as a technical analyst so I did my work from home. My home office had a gorgeous view and I could look out over the mountains onto the valley. Sunny liked to come into the house every hour or so to check on me so I would leave the door from the mudroom open just enough for him to enter and he would come in, get a loving pat and then return to his job of patrolling the area or just lay on the porch to sun himself (he had a rough life). He had his freedom and came and went at his leisure - except at night. When the sun went down he was locked in his condo - to be released the next morning. There were many predators on the mountain at night and I wanted to protect him. He was perfectly content to lay in his warm bed and have food and water to consume.

When my work day ended, Sunny and I would take a daily walk all the way up over the ridge and back down. He would lay on top of the deck railing when he felt the time had come for me to cease work and give him some attention. He loved our walks and that was a daily routine for us. Since I never had a cat as a pet, I really wasn't aware of their patterns and traits. One day I was telling my daughter of the adventures of Sunny and Tara - trekking through the mountains - and she said, "Mom...are you aware that cats don't normally like taking walks like dogs do?" We laughed but I never really thought about that preconceived notion. All I knew was that Sunny and I enjoyed our long walks.

Sunny was very curious about the deer who came into the yard when I offered corn and apples. Mule deer are magnificent beings with big antler racks. There was a herd of about 7 or 8 who came into the yard every morning. And..they were a bit territorial since their delicious buffet was offered there. One day Sunny was sitting in the yard and the deer came down over the ridge for their breakfast at Cafe Tara. Sunny started up the ridge to meet one young buck who I named Uhtred.

Uhtred started towards Sunny so he stopped. The deer kept advancing – not in a charge...but steady. I think he was just curious about this cat. Sunny was always protective of me and stood his ground so the deer came right up to him and nudged his head. At that point, I guess Sunny thought he may want to move since the deer had a few pounds on him.

Standing his ground against a deer many times his size may have seemed foolish, but that was the nature of Sunny. He was a warrior then and even at the end.

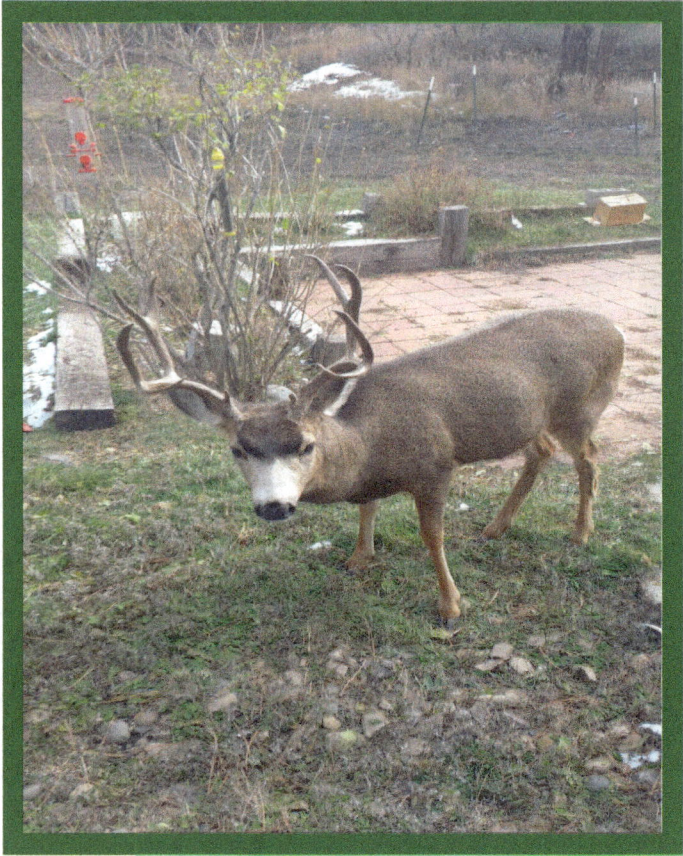

Clark was Family

CLARK

I loved all the deer in Pagosa Springs but Clark was the one who captured my heart. It was obvious from the moment I met Clark that he and I would be friends. He wasn't afraid to come close and would walk right up to me and wait for my apple offering. He would never take food from my hand, although, for some reason, I never tried to coax him to do so. Clark played the role of Military Captain in his herd and would enter an area first to make sure it was safe for the General. Then when he felt it was safe the alpha leader entered. All the males in this particular herd had at least 8-point racks and were extremely majestic. I would go out into the yard and offer them corn, apples and vegetables. One morning, as I stood among them, I realized that I was surrounded by a whole lot of artillery. Standing in the middle of these mature bucks with a lot of protection on their heads made me realize that not only did they trust me completely but I also trusted them. I have read that male deer can be very aggressive and temperamental during mating season but I never saw any aggression in these deer friends. All I saw was beauty and appreciation.

Clark would hang around with me during the evening hours and sometimes I would see him resting peacefully in my yard in the evening- only to find him there when the sun came up. I guess he wanted to get early access to the tasty morsels I offered in the morning. It's probably clear to you by now that I loved Clark very much.

It was now spring time and many afternoons a doe and her twin fawns would rest in the shade of the Juniper tree in the backyard. I enjoyed watching the fawns jump and play in the yard...they were so funny. I had a big tub filled with fresh water in the yard as an offering so the animals could quench their thirst. I also had a bird bath for the birds and Sunny to drink from. The fawns loved to play in the water so they would jump into the big tub and splash around...one of the funniest things I ever saw. I sat and laughed at them for as long as they played. One day a fawn drank out of the bird bath and Sunny wasn't putting up with that. He jumped down from his perch on the deck banister and ran out to meet the offender. The fawn just saw Sunny as another playmate so he proceeded with his playtime. Sunny's grumpy disposition didn't dissuade the fawn - he just wanted to play. Soon Sunny was tired of this punk kid's antics and walked off to rest in the little lean-to tent I built for him to shelter him from the intense sun while he rested in the afternoon.

One afternoon Clark mosied into the yard while the doe and twins were resting in the shade. I was very interested in what would take place next. Would the doe jump up and dash out of the yard when Clark entered? Would Clark chase the young ones away? Would there be a stand-off between Clark and a female protecting her young?

I watched with great interest. The whole scene seemed to be in slow motion. Clarke entered the yard like he owned it...comfortable and entitled. He paid no attention to the doe and her young but I could tell that he was very aware of them. The doe didn't move...she rested in the cool grass but the two fawns jumped up and ran over to Clark. Clark ignored them. They began playing in the tub of water - as normal. Finally, they ran up to Clark and wanted to play. They would nip at his knees and feet and he just looked at them like a human father trying to get some yard work done while the kids were constantly bugging him. And...the doe wasn't at all concerned that her babies were agitating a 10-point buck. This went on for an hour. Finally, I realized that this was Clark's family...his mate and children. From that point on, they got together often in my backyard and it was a beautiful sight to behold. Clark and his family spending time with me - precious.

Clark's Kids

Fat Lady in a Girdle – Looks alot like me, Hee Hee

SUNNY IN SCOTTSDALE AND BACK TO THE MOUNTAINS

Having a rental property in Scottsdale, Arizona is a blessing...and a curse. For those of you who have never visited Scottsdale....let's put it this way...there is a lot of wealth in that city - especially in the northern part of town. Scottsdale and Phoenix overflow into one another and there are lovely parts of Phoenix but many times people move to Scottsdale because of the status.

The unique aspect of my house is that it's zoned for horses. This property is very rare and unique because it allows horses in the City of Scottsdale. In fact, they call the area the magic mile because you are in the middle of Scottsdale, have Phoenix taxes (which are lower) and the houses are afforded larger lots and are considered "horse property". As you can imagine, this property is very attractive to those who own horses – two horses could comfortably inhabit the acre of land.

I've rented to several people with horses and they always took very good care of the property but this last time I made a big mistake renting to some younger people who had two big dogs...almost as big as horses! Now I was faced with having to go back to Scottsdale to evict them and also prepare the house for the next tenants. I couldn't leave Sunny in the mountains by himself, although he obviously knew how to take care of himself. But...since that fateful winter day when we met, I considered him my responsibility as well as my friend. So, he was coming with me. I doubted that he had ever been out of a rural area and the sounds and hustle and bustle of Scottsdale would probably freak him out but I was ready to take the chance rather than leave him to fend for himself for several weeks.

I found a cat carrier to transport him in – thinking it would be better to have him contained to one area of my car rather than roaming freely at his will. So in the carrier he went and back to Scottsdale we headed. He was a nightmare in the carrier. He whined and cried for hours – biting at the mesh of the cage like a wildcat (that he actually was). Finally, after hours of agony on both our parts, I opened the carrier and to my surprise, he laid down on the passenger seat and went to sleep. All I could think of was...why did I put both of us through this? I should have taken the more positive approach first and if that didn't work, THEN put him in the carrier. Well...what can I say.

After I removed Sunny from the carrier and had some peace and quiet, I thought alot about Merlin and how he was. Should I contact him when in Scottsdale? Was he still in a relationship? I had no phone number for him so the only way I could contact him was to call his place of employment. Should I do that? Really, Tara...if he wants to talk to you, he has your phone number. I was still very hurt and confused about why he betrayed me but I guess he had his reasons.

All of my life, I've had an extraordinary ability to manifest what I wanted in my life. This was one time that the situation was out of my control. I wanted to be with him ....or did I? Did I really? Perhaps this trip back to Scottsdale wasn't about Merlin but about me. Perhaps I had a life lesson to learn. Perhaps I just needed a break from the harsh winter in the Pagosa Springs. It would be beautifully mild in Scottsdale right now (in January) so enjoy it girl!

When we arrived at the house, I pulled into the garage and closed the door so Sunny wouldn't be traumatized by a new environment and try to escape. The first thing he did was to jump on the roof of the car and try to crawl up into the attic of the garage...almost gave me a heart attack. Once I got him in the house, he stood frozen in the living room and then tried to climb up the inside of the chimney...once again...heart attack time. How in the world would we ever have gotten him out. I closed off the chimney area and breathed another sigh of relief. Were there any more potential hazards for this cat? I guess we would see. One thing for sure...I didn't want this guy outside in the yard. What in the world would I do if he got outside the house and I couldn't retrieve him?

Finally Sunny calmed down and made his permanent residence in the master bathroom - in the corner of the vanity. How strange...but that was fine. I set up his bed and toys there in the bathroom.

It was so surreal to return to a place that felt very much like home (because it was my home for many years) but it was in an area that was as alien to me as Mars. If I could have just picked up the house and moved it to Colorado...I would have been so happy. The house was perfect for me and had an office for my work. The outside was so beautiful with a large back porch and sizable piece of land. Even though Scottsdale is surrounded by the very unique Sonoran Desert, my back yard looked like I resided on the east coast - very lush and green and lovely. My friend, Kim, once said that this yard had a perfect eco-balance and I should be proud of what I had created. It was so simple...I created what I love. When I moved into the house, the entire outside was just red dirt - nothing more. I planted grass (which wasn't easy in a desert that had clay soil as hard as a rock). But patience won over. I had a good sized garden that was still producing long after I left, honeysuckle bushes, herbs gracing the flower beds of the yard, sunflowers for the birds to eat and my beautiful huge pine tree in the back yard that graciously shaded most of the top tier of the property. I absolutely love that tree. It took on the hot summers of Arizona and saved me and my property from being scorched by the sun. It also provided a place for my friend Serena and I to bond and helped all the creatures on the property to make it through the summer.

I wondered if Serena (my hawk friend) was still in the neighborhood and if I would see Spencer (my hummingbird friend). Spencer had taken me through some tough times when I first broke up with Merlin...I hoped he was well.

Sunny was having a tense time trying to acclimate to the new surroundings. He was used to patrolling the perimeter of the house many times a day but now he was stuck inside. I was intent on getting the necessary maintenance done and having new renters take over the house as soon as possible so this guy could regain his normal patterns - in Pagosa Springs. In the meantime, I would enjoy the beautiful Arizona winter.

Most days I worked hard all day and then spent some time outside in the evenings. I had only been in Scottsdale about 3 or 4 days when I saw a hummingbird land on the agave bush next to my porch. He looked familiar and he was gazing at me like he knew me...unafraid. Oh my

Lord...it was Spencer. We were both so excited to see each other again and it was a surprise to me that he recognized me after being away for a bit. Our relationship picked up where it left off. The next day I bought a hummingbird feeder and we spent evenings together on the porch. I started feeling bad that Sunny was left out so I decided to put him on his leash connected to a harness (to keep him in the yard) and see how he liked it outside. He hated it! He was so freaked out that I ushered him back inside where he felt comfortable.

After a couple of weeks in Scottsdale, I rented the house to a nice couple and sadly and tearfully said goodbye to Spencer once again and Sunny and I hopped in the car (without the cat carrier...I might add) and began the long trip home to the mountains of Pagosa Springs, Colorado. This time, Sunny rested quietly and comfortably on the front seat of the car with me - not even a peep out of him.

Finally, Sunny and I headed for home but there was one stop before we made it home - Tara Mandala, which is a Buddhist Retreat Center in the mountains outside of Pagosa Springs. My Spiritual Guide told me this was the perfect time for my first visit. I didn't know why but felt the answer would be revealed soon enough.

Tara Mandala sits high in the San Juan Mountains. When you stand at the highest part (where the temple sits), you can look out over the entire valley. It feels like you are on top of the world. This thought took me back to the trip I took to Tibet when I accompanied my Buddhist Teacher to take medicine to the nomadic tribes who inhabited his region. His monastery stood very high in the Himalayan Mountains and standing on the roof of that structure and looking down over the valley gave me that same feeling. Eagles and ravens would soar by me so close I felt I could fly right along with them.

I didn't hear any human voices when I entered the Tara Mandala Temple so I thought it was empty. I wandered around the building - meandering through the halls of the first and second floor. It was beautiful. I had seen enough and was ready to leave but my Spiritual Guide told me to remain and led me to the entrance of the main temple hall. I opened the door and saw there were a group of people sitting in the middle of the hall so I quickly closed the doors and turned to leave.

My Guide stopped me and told me to go inside. I didn't want to....I would be disturbing the group who were already in the hall. But I knew I had to enter so I did so quietly and sat down to listen to what these people were discussing. It turns out that this was a Dharma class with two Teachers and about ten students. As I listened I was shocked at how elementary the teachings were. I thought back to my first Buddhist Teacher and the teachings she gave to us every Sunday morning. I had learned much from her and had also learned alot from my second Buddhist Teacher - a Rinpoche (which means "Precious One").

When the teaching ended, one of the Teachers came over to talk to me. I was interested in knowing how long these students had been learning Buddhism and she told me these were the senior students and had been studying for over 8 years. We ended our conversation and I sat in the Buddha Hall wondering how it could be that I learned what these students were being taught my first year of study. I felt extremely fortunate.

My eyes caught movement so I shifted my gaze to the main statue of Tara Bodhisattva at the front of the temple. She was huge - a story tall and there were 21 smaller Tara statues around the perimeter of the temple. Quite extravagant and beautiful. I felt very at ease and peaceful and just closed my eyes to meditate. All of a sudden, I heard a voice calling me. My eyes flipped open but saw no one. Then I heard the voice again and it was coming from the large statue of Tara. Was I having an auditory hallucination?

Tara Bodhisattva began to speak to me and thanked me for the teachings that I was about to give. What teachings?....I thought. I had given two human students some classes in Free the Mind while I was in Scottsdale but I hadn't given classes since. Tara told me that I would teach Free the Mind in the mountains of Colorado and the trees would carry the message "far and wide".

Tara instructed me to step outside the temple – which I did. The front of the temple entrance looked down over the valley for as far as I could see. I realized what I was to do. I felt the energy rising from my core and into my heart. I spread my arms and the energy flew from my fingers like a sparkling mist. When it hit the pine trees in front of the temple, they began to glisten. Soon the energy spread to all the trees on the mountain.

As you may remember, my Spiritual Guide explained to me that trees have the magical ability to carry a spiritual message for great distances. One tree will "pass it on" to the next so that I would have my teaching message traveling all across the country because the trees would spread the word. I was so overwhelmed and humbled to be a part of this amazing experience that I wept. At that moment, I realized that my teachings would touch so many beings – whether they be human, animal, magical or others. I saw my destiny in those trees.

As I approached the car, Sunny was standing up in the driver's seat waiting for me. I could tell the energy touched him as well. He was standing there anticipating what would come next. WOW...What a day, I thought....and I shared it with my comrade who came to me from the mountains and drilled his way into my heart. What would come next? Only heaven knows!

BACK TO OUR DAILY ROUTINE:

Once we got back to Pagosa Springs, we settled into our daily routine. Sunny and I meshed like an old married couple who had lived together for 50 years. We would take a short walk around the immediate vicinity of the house in the mornings and then in the evenings, we walked the entire ridge which would take about an hour. He seemed to enjoy the walks and the animals we met. But any small rodent was seen as a tasty morsel and he would go after them like he was starving. To me this was just "cat nature" and a habit since he had taken care of himself in the mountains before we met. This behavior wasn't something I cared for since I don't like to see animals injured but it was in HIS nature to hunt and it wasn't MY business to try to change that. He would bring birds, moles, lizards and other beings into the house to present to me and I must say...I understood why he did it but wasn't having any of it.

One evening we were taking our routine route up over the ridge when all of a sudden, Sunny sat down and began to whine. I had only heard this sound one other time - when he first came onto my porch and needed help right before the snowstorm.

I was at a loss as to why he was behaving like this but the hair stood up on my body and I've learned that when this happens....BEWARE! I patted him to calm him down and even held him a bit but he was intent on not taking another step forward into the mountains. I looked all around and couldn't see any danger but I trusted Sunny and myself and realized we needed to turn back and return to the house....quickly. After all, this was not Scottsdale and there were cougars, bears, coyotes and wolves in the mountains so best to be too cautious rather than not cautious enough.

As I spun around to retreat to the house, I looked down and saw two sets of animal tracks in the fresh mud: one was a cougar and the other a wolf ....both moving in the same direction. It seemed strange to see two predators moving simultaneously. Or...was it that one was tracking the other. My instincts told me not to rationalize but to leave so I turned to

Sunny and said, "OK...Bud, let's go home." That cat took off like a bat out of hell. And, I followed him. I never moved so fast on the ridge with all the rocks and crevices but that day I moved through the familiar terrain like a clumsy gazelle. When Sunny and I made it to the porch, we were both spent and happy to be home. I wondered if I would ever feel comfortable enough to go back out into the mountains again. It was clear that Sunny's early warning signal alerted me to the danger. The fear I felt that night disappeared as soon as the next evening came and it was time to walk the ridge with my comrade.

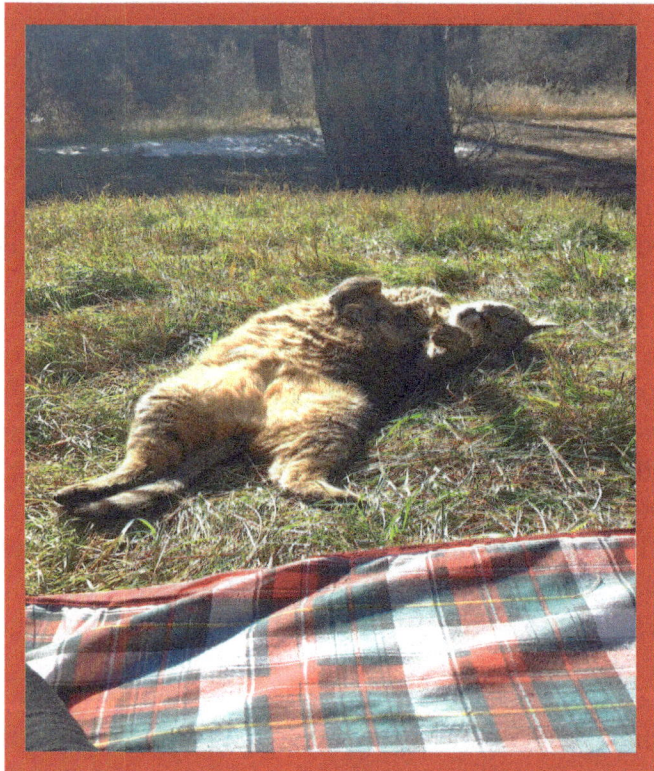

Sunny Really Knew How to Relax

Sunny and I had a tradition of lounging in the sun at lunch time. I remember that even in the winter time, we would spread a blanket over the snow and sit in the yard to catch some rays. A couple days after the incident on the ridge we were taking advantage of a beautiful day - the sun was bright and the cloudless sky was blue - a perfect day in Colorado. I was lying face up with my eyes closed (of course) and Sunny was sleeping beside me. Suddenly, I sensed a being flying over me. I sensed how it cast a shadow over the sun. When I jumped up, Sunny had already gotten to his feet. Looking up, I saw a Vulture flying over us. Holy Moly! All I could think of was, "We better move or that vulture will think we're dead and swoop down on us!" By this time, Sunny had already made his way back to the porch. I thought to myself, "Dorothy....you are no longer in Kansas!"

The next morning was Saturday so there was no work. I was able to leisurely sit on the porch and then go about my day with my comrade by my side. As I sipped my tea, I wondered what adventures we would have today. Heaven knows we've had some interesting times lately.

I contemplated on why I had given up the city to come to the wilderness? Why did I leave convenience behind to live as a "mountain woman" who no longer got pedicures, haircuts and facials? Gently, my Spiritual Guide answered my questions, "Tara...you are fulfilling your destiny. That's why you're here. When walking the spiritual path, it's necessary to slow your life down so that you have the space in your mind to realize what is important. People may believe that pursuing a career to make a good living, getting married, raising children and retiring in Florida are their life goals but that's not so. The true reason beings come to this life is to work out their karma....not create more. Most people, however, are too busy with their outer, physical lives to contemplate on their inner being (their Buddha Nature which is the Pure Mind.)"

She continued, "Your journey is to experience your own spiritual path, to realize who you truly are, to contemplate the resolution of your physical condition, and to teach others who have an open mind to do the same." I realized her words were true because I had already begun teaching Free the Mind in Scottsdale. But now I knew why I was here on the mountain and my mind was at peace. I had no idea how and when this whole scenario would unfold but I was sure I had agreed to take on this mission - even before my birth. So, here I was - walking my spiritual path with my friend, Sunny.

I looked out over the majestic pines that lined the ridge and my yard. How beautiful they were. Snow had just fallen the evening before and the sun's rays peeking over the ridge brought a sparkly aliveness to the trees - like a winter wonderland. Suddenly my eyes caught movement. I saw vapor or a smoke-like substance coming from one of the pine trees near my house. First, I thought it was just the snow vaporizing as a result of the sun's rays hitting the snow. I looked at the other trees in the back yard - no vapor. I gazed at the tree beside the one that emitted the vapor. Nothing. No other tree was emitting this substance. I was so curious. Then my guide whispered, "Tara...that is magic! "Magic?", I asked. She continued, "Yes...this is the physical manifestation of magic. As I stated earlier, trees are magical beings. They can calm you, take care of you, and heal you. They can even carry messages from one tree to another so that the message can be carried for thousands of miles. They will help you carry your message to many beings who are not physically present in your teachings."

I sat there a long time totally in awe of what I saw and what my Spiritual Guide told me. Why me? This teaching that I was to share sounded important. The journey had already begun whether I was ready or not.

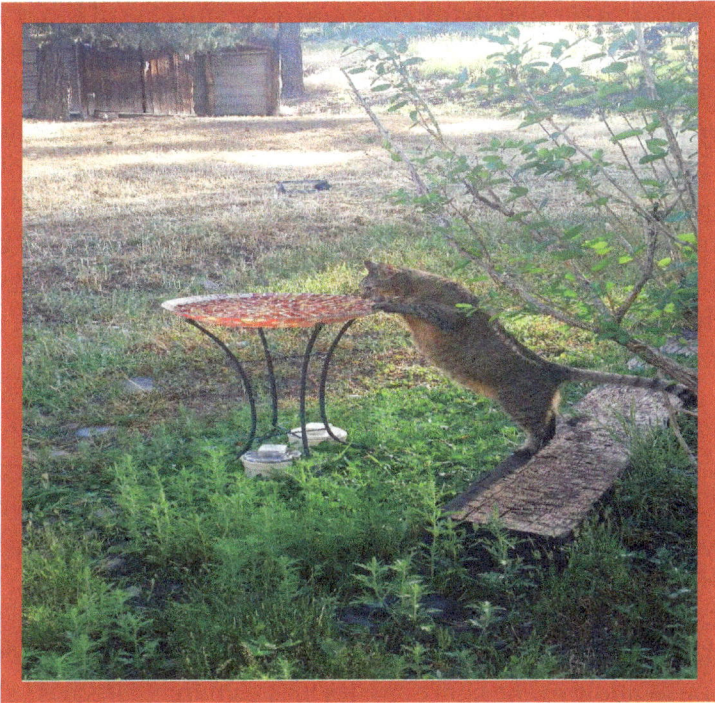

Sunny's Bird Bath

Sunny had two (not one but two) bowls at his disposal with clear, fresh water in them but he chose to drink from the bird bath. He liked to do things his way but wasn't so rigid that he refused to compromise with me and he did that because he loved me. He had a lovely and grumpy personality. He knew what he wanted and he would insist on it...but he was never cruel and he was usually very sweet to me.

I stored peanuts in the closet of the mudroom and noticed a squirrel came into the room and helped himself to peanuts from time to time. I had no issue with that BUT one day the squirrel came into the mudroom and met Sunny the protector at the door when he was exiting the closet. There was wrestling, squealing, and lots of activity. Neither one was hurt but the end result was that Sunny was isolated in the bathroom and the squirrel was incarcerated in my bedroom. I had no idea of how to capture this fat squirrel but I decided the only way to succeed was to use a bird net. As I chased him around my bedroom, he ran across my bed 3 or 4 times - which I wasn't crazy about. Finally, I captured him in the net and dragged him gently out the door - freeing him outside. The whole time I was rounding this squirrel up, Sunny was yodeling in the guest bathroom. Not a happy camper. I certainly got my workout that day. Interestingly enough, that incident didn't really deter the squirrel much because he showed up again the next day looking for peanuts in the mudroom closet.

Since I normally left the room to the mudroom open for Sunny to come in and out during the day, there tended to be creatures coming into the house and then getting trapped there. This house had cathedral ceilings which made it really hard to capture birds and release them...that's why I had the bird net.

One day a humming bird got trapped in my house and was fluttering around the window in the bedroom. He was a young male and very beautiful and was confused as to why he could see the outside world but he couldn't get there. When I saw him fluttering and scared, I was concerned that it would be difficult to spring him from his prison. I walked gently up to the window and when he saw me, he immediately sat down on the windowsill. I approached him and scooped him up in my hands. As I gently carried him outside, his little beak was sticking out between my fingers and I fell in love with this little guy.

If you ever have the opportunity to hold a hummingbird in your hands, consider yourself very fortunate because holding these amazing beings is like holding fairy dust. Their energy is extremely refined and they vibrate at a level you will never forget. I took him outside and opened my hands. He sat in my hand and studied me - like he didn't really want to fly off but finally he did. This is a memory that will never fade from my consciousness and I will hold dear.

As I already stated, when you live on the side of a mountain and leave your door open, expect wild visitors. They are very curious. I forgot to close the door to the mudroom one day when Sunny and I went on a hike and found hoof prints in the mudroom floor when we returned. I guess Clark wanted an apple and thought he could fetch it for himself!

One summer afternoon as I was working, I heard Sunny's food bowl rattling in the mudroom and I thought nothing of it since this was about the time in midmorning when he would be having a snack. All of a sudden, I heard commotion and scuffling. I jumped up and ran out to see Sunny and a baby skunk rolling around on the deck...what the heck! The skirmish ended with the baby skunk scampering out through the yard and Sunny sitting on the porch hissing. Interesting, I thought, that the skunk didn't spray. THAT would have been bad....real bad. My reasoning was that perhaps baby skunks this guy's age may not have their "stink" defense in place until older. OH CONTRAIRE! I researched to find that baby skunks are armed with their odor system from birth. Maybe this little guy didn't use his odor because he didn't feel the need. Sunny didn't hurt him....but warned him not to be chomping down on food that wasn't offered to him.

Interestingly, I had a whole family of skunks living under the barn not 20 yards from the house. In fact, I regularly offered them vegetable cuttings for their dinner. Not once did they spray around the house. In fact, the only time I smelled the odor de skunk was when the neighbor's dog got too close to a family member. This proves to me that when we treat wildlife as friends rather than a nuisance, they respond with the same respect for us.

Another of Sunny and Tara's escapades included a bear. It was a delightful evening much like other summer evenings in Colorado. I was talking with my mother over the phone and Sunny was stretching out in the cool grass. I saw movement out of the corner of my eye and watched a beautiful cinnamon colored black bear coming down over the mountain. The bear, Sunny and I were in perfect alignment and so

Sunny was directly between the bear and myself. I panicked a bit because you just never know what a bear will do and he was big enough to do mortal damage to both Sunny and myself. I was stunned by this bear's beauty but I also had protective instincts to take care of my friend, Sunny. I began yelling and waving my hands so that the bear knew I was on the porch. He did not retreat. At this point, the bear was only about 25 yards away from Sunny and he wasn't changing his course. And, why was Sunny just laying there? He should have been long-gone by now.

Remember...I was on the phone with my Mother. I know that she's happy that I'm living in a beautiful place that I love but she worries also that there are lots of predators in the mountains of Colorado and she fears for my safety.

For a moment I forgot I was on the phone having a mother-daughter conversation. I saw the bear getting closer and closer to Sunny so I started screaming at the top of my lungs....Sunny didn't move. Finally I ran out into the yard and scooped that lazy cat up in my arms. The bear thought I was charging him so he turned and hightailed it up over the mountain. Poor guy....I scared him half to death which was unfortunate. Through all of this in the end, I had Sunny in my arms and the phone was cradled between my chin and my hunched up shoulder. Needless to say, my Mom heard everything and it must have been unbearably frightening for her to think I may be injured. So...some of us were frightened that day...but not Sunny.

Sunny was a warrior...to the end. He became ill and died in my arms right before I left Pagosa Springs in 2016 and I miss him every single day. I buried him on the mountain because I thought that is what he would have wanted. I am so appreciative to Sunny for all the love, devotion and comradery he shared with me. Life with him is the reason my view of cats has changed. I will love him and cherish our time together for the rest of my life. Thank you Sunny...

TREES

Do you like sitting under a tree to relax and rejuvenate? Have you wondered why you chose to sit under a tree rather than on your porch or in the grass and you felt so much better afterwards? We would have to search far and wide for a person who hates trees. Why? Because trees embody universal wisdom and they will take negative emotions from us and recycle them into the air.

That may sound hokey...right? But it is the truth.

I pretty much took trees for granted until 15 years ago when I was living in a condo in the middle of Scottsdale. There were lots of trees in the condo community and one eucalyptus shaded my front deck. One day I noticed it was dying so I contacted the maintenance people to report it. It took them 8 days to fix the drip system and I sure wasn't going to let that tree die so I started hauling buckets of water out to the porch and pouring it on the tree's root system - hoping to save the tree. By the time the maintenance folks got around to fixing the drip system that watered the tree, it had fully recuperated.

This may sound strange but the tree showed its appreciation to me in a way that I cannot explain and never experienced. It's limbs and leaves cradled my deck with shade and I could feel that it wanted to be closer to me. When I moved from the condo, I was sad to lose my relationship with the tree and even went back a couple times to visit. If this story sounds like it happened during an acid trip that's only because you haven't had a caring relationship with a tree or you weren't aware that a tree was extending itself to you. Once you have that relationship, your life will never be the same.

The next experience I had with a tree was in the house I purchased after leaving the condo - my Scottsdale house. There was only one tree in the backyard and it was a huge, beautiful pine...obviously female by the looks of its curves. I soon noted that every single person who came into my yard- whether they were a friend, family member or stranger, commented on its beauty and magnificence. It sheltered and protected the entire house, most of the yard and me.

It wasn't long before I enjoyed a beautiful relationship with that tree. I would lay under it for hours talking with Serena, my hawk friend. It housed and protected many birds, insects and unseen beings like wood nymphs, gnomes, sprites, and tree spirits. Yes...those beings are mythical AND they do exist if you understand how to see and communicate to them. I gave several spiritual teachings to those tree spirits when I was in the house on the side of the mountain in Pagosa Springs and also in Dolores.

Talking about trees reminds me of my days of studying Buddhism and I recalled that the Buddha sat under the Bodhi tree to become enlightened. I guess I assumed that he had nowhere else to sit that provided shelter - since he lived outside. But now I realize the real reason was that trees protect and shelter us and they embrace us like no other being. They are selfless and give totally to others - without a thought for themselves. Many important historical events took place in the presence of trees. We have all learned that trees provide us with our most important need...oxygen. If we don't have that element, we are dead in a few minutes. And most important and beneficial herbal and pharmaceutical health remedies are extracted from plants and trees in the rain forests.

In Pagosa Springs trees lined all the mountain ridges.There was an amazing juniper tree on the top of the ridge behind my house that was old and gnarly...and it was the picture of ancient wisdom. When Sunny and I took our walks I would stand with my back against the tree and ask it questions. It gave me the most thoughtful answers. Some of you may believe that really the answers came from me and the tree was just my conduit. That's possible. But either way, wisdom and comfort came through...and that was important for me.

I remember one cool evening in Colorado: Sunny and I were sitting in the yard and enjoying the crisp air. I had experienced a rough day. Being in love can be tough on its own but unrequited love is brutal. I was sad and weeping a bit and when I looked up, the tree across the yard appeared to be opening its arms to me. I really couldn't believe my eyes but I definitely saw movement in that Juniper tree. Sunny even saw the same and jumped to his feet.

I watched in amazement as the tree opened its arms and held me in its embrace. I never felt so safe and comforted in my entire life. The experience didn't last long. It didn't need to. I thanked the tree for being there for me and all the rest of the trees near me said, "Tara...we are all here for you when you need us." I was so shocked and elated to hear all their voices proclaiming their desire to help in any way they could. At first, I considered that I may be losing my mind...voices in the head...if you know what I mean.

But soon, I realized they were all so lovely and just wanted to help. I had so many beings supporting me here on the mountainside. I asked myself, "How can you be lonely with all these friends with you every step of the way? They are always here to protect you, to comfort and love you."

Young Male Mule Deer in Velvet– "The Boys"

LEAVING PAGOSA

Sunny and I had spent two winters and summers in Pagosa Springs and we knew how to navigate our lives in this big house. Every time I walked past the mother-in-law quarters, I would think of Merlin and how I picked this house so that we would have enough space for two alphas. But, in the end...all was fine. I had my house on the mountain with a good friend who loved me. I was surrounded by magical pine trees and my wild friends like Clark and Uhtred the deer, the family of skunks who lived under the barn, the hummingbirds, and many beautiful birds and occasional furry visitors like squirrels, weasels and wild turkey (whom I never saw but heard almost every day.

I'll never forget that fateful day when the property manager I worked with to rent this house showed up at my door. She was cheerful...but forcibly so. "How's it going, Tara?" I saw right through her happy demeanor and asked what was wrong. She knew I wouldn't take what she had to tell me well. "The people who own the house want to sell it. Are you interested in buying it?" I really liked the house but it was way too big for me alone - especially to buy. Also, it was built mostly as a summer home. The wood stove in the living room didn't heat the place sufficiently but the auxiliary gas heater was very expensive to use and didn't heat the house well either. Also the cathedral ceiling in the living room forced all the heat to the second floor - where I spent very little time. Even when the wood stove was running in full force, the first story was still cold and I always wore 3 layers of clothing in the winter. So,to rent...loved this house. To buy.....there were too any negatives.

I was sad...I wasn't ready to leave Clark, I was concerned that Sunny would freak out in a new place AND...I would have to find a place to live that had a separate residence for him because I did have an allergy to cat dander (so I didn't want to push it too much). It was July of 2016 and I had 4 months before I had to move. Sometimes it seemed like a good amount of time and others, it seemed like no time at all. Once the house was being shown by realtors, I knew I had to make some plans. So, I began working with a realtor to find a house to buy. There were several nice houses but they were in the wilderness and the internet reception wasn't strong enough to support my work. 33 houses later, the realtor and I were both exhausted. My biggest concern was Sunny and I asked my Spiritual Guide to..well...guide me. She informed me that Sunny would not be leaving this mountain when I left. That news made me even sadder.

By September, Sunny had been diagnosed with diabetes and some other physical issues. As hard as the veterinarian tried to save him and as much as I tried to heal him, Sunny passed away in my arms in late September. My friend had passed and my heart was broken. I was very grateful for the time we had together but I was so sad that he was no longer with me. I cried for weeks.

If all of this wasn't bad enough, I was notified by my employer that I was being laid off from my job. In my entire career as a technical analyst and computer programmer, I had never been fired, laid off, and never even received a bad work review. Why was this happening to me? I lost my house on the mountains , I had lost my beloved companion, and now I had lost my job - my livelihood. I was angry and hurt and just beside myself.

Since Sunny was gone and I had 6 months severance pay coming from the company who heartlessly and unjustifiably laid me off, I decided to rent a small condo in the town of Pagosa Springs for the time being until I could heal a bit from all the pain and regroup to figure out what to do and where to go. I had no family here in Pagosa and only a couple of friends so not much support system. I knew I wouldn't be happy in a condo that was located within the town limits of Pagosa Springs - cooped up without a yard and trees. There were apartments I could rent in town but that would be worse than the condo on the outskirts of town. There were absolutely no rentals similar to the one I was leaving and I wasn't even sure I should stay in Pagosa any longer.

I didn't feel like it...but I had to pack up my things. I had been working all day and needed to take a break. It was so strange living in this house without Sunny and as I sat on the porch with the hummingbirds buzzing my head, I thought of him. Suddenly I heard a loud bang....a gunshot. It was deer season (the worst time of my life in Pagosa) and I ran to the deck. There in the neighbor's yard I saw a beautiful 12-point buck - one of the deer I offered corn and apples to in the winter laying still in the grass. "What the hell!", I thought. I walked across the road - not yet knowing what I was going to say...or scream...but it wouldn't be pretty. I was sure that the wrathful deity in me was sure to come out.

I knew these folks and their boys. The husband helped plow my driveway in the winter months. I liked them until today. I knocked on the door and the mother came to greet me sweetly. I said, "Are you aware that someone shot a deer in your yard?" She said....very joyfully...like it was a great thing, "Oh, yeah - my son shot it. It's deer season and he has a license."

I began by asking her how she could be so cruel to such a beautiful animal and to her son. I asked why she thought it was OK for her 16 year old boy to kill without giving it much of a thought. Secondly, it was against the law to shoot in one's back yard - with houses well within range. The gloves were off! She told me she was sorry that I felt the way I did and I told her I was sorry I ever spent time with her family. All the while the son was standing behind her listening to the confrontation. Somehow, I knew this was all for the son's benefit. He had lived in a family who shot deer and ate the meat every year - much like my family in Pennsylvania. His mind had been molded by his culture just as you and I have been molded by ours. I hope that my view I shared with him and his mother gave him a new perspective. Perhaps one day he will think back to this incident and realize that wild animals are not here on this earth for human benefit. They are here just as humans are - to work out karma and hopefully reach some realization. Little did he and his mother know that the majestic being he just killed was superior to him (spiritually). If he would have realized that, I wonder if he would have pulled the trigger without a second thought.

As I walked across the road back to my house - knowing I was done with Pagosa Springs. I could no longer live in a place....in a group of people who think nothing of taking a life. This is inbred in the people here - generation after generation and few have the insight to question these practices....and cruelties. As beautiful as Pagosa Springs was, I was done with it. Unless I had 100 acres of land and it was all fenced and posted that there was no hunting allowed, I would never live here again. Where was I to go where the mountains were so beautiful and hunting wasn't considered a favorite sport?

So, in a week or so I was off to the condo to lick my wounds....and what deep wounds they were. I began applying for jobs online but knew the chance was slim that I would find a job similar to the one I lost and still be able to work remotely. The thought of having to go into an office and work a job again after working from home for 5 years was excruciatingly painful. I put a lot of effort into finding a job but most of my time was spent on contemplating why all of this happened and what was in store for me in the next phase of my life. I had only done a few teachings the entire time I lived in Pagosa Springs. Was it because I was healing from losing my relationship with Merlin? Was it because I wasn't in a place I was destined to teach? Was it because I wasn't ready to teach? Or...was it because I wasn't good enough...to be a Spiritual Teacher? I had a lot to contemplate and had all the time in the world!

I knew there was one being I had to carefully say goodbye to and that was Clark the deer. Clark and I had grown very close and we connected with one another on a heart level. How would I explain to him that I was leaving and, more importantly, how would I explain that he must never come back to this house again after I leave? I had no idea if the people who purchased this house were hunters and had no idea if Clark was in danger or not. So I tried connecting to him to explain that I was leaving (sadly) and he should never come back here again...if he had been in the neighbors yard that day the shot was fired, it could have been him lying dead on the ground.

The next day, Clark came for apples. I guess my attempt to communicate to him had failed or he was stubborn. I tried another tactic. I started yelling and screaming and chased him out of the yard and up over the ridge. This was inspired by the movie *Dances with Wolves*. That didn't work either. He just looked at me as if I lost my mind. Nothing worked so I stopped offering apples to him and tried to explain again. It broke my heart to treat him this way but it was in an attempt to save his life.

When I left the house on the mountain, I cried for days over leaving my tree friends, animal friends, hummingbird friends and Clark. They and

Sunny were such a huge part of my life. And...although I realized Sunny was never meant to leave the mountain, I felt a great loss when he went to his next life and left me without my companion - my comrade.

As I placed the last item in the moving truck, I turned to take in one last look at my friends who had brought me such joy and comfort over the last two years. Suddenly, the trees started sparkling as I said my final goodbye to them. I heard the big pine in the back of the house say, "We trees can communicate for thousands of miles. One tree tells the next and on and on. All you have to do is communicate with any tree in your yard and have the intention of communicating with us, and we will hear you. We will always be with you and will be there to help in any way we can - and to pass on your teachings far and wide."

I was first shocked that I could hear the tree's message and also wondered what it meant by "we will spread your teachings far and wide?" I guessed that I was to embark on a new phase in my life. Would I be teaching? Would I teach in the condo? Doubted it. This experience totally blew me away. How can a tree in Colorado communicate with a tree in Pennsylvania? The answer to both of these questions - One word: MAGIC.

LIVING A LIFE OF AWARENESS....SEEING THE MAGIC

I had just moved into a furnished condo (and put my belongings into storage). It was October and the weather was beautiful but I had no way to enjoy it. When I lived on the mountain, I would go out onto the porch with Sunny and enjoy the morning. We watched the hummingbirds buzzing my head, observed the birds and rabbits hunting for breakfast, and offered apples to Clark when he ventured into the yard. But now there were no wild animals except for the really plump and cute raccoons who would come for scraps at night. There were too many people in one area - too many for my taste and I had only a tiny yard. It was crowded. I was grateful for a place to stay but not happy at all with the surroundings.

I continued applying for jobs but my heart just wasn't into it. So I decided to just relax and take time – time for myself. Time that I never took before – not in 61 years. I was still living in Pagosa Springs at the time and it was so beautiful. I decided to witness the majesty of the mountainside without the boundaries of having to do a job.

I thought back to the morning on the porch when I saw the vapor arising from inside the pine tree in my backyard. What an amazing experience it was. I remember my Spiritual Guide telling me that we can see magic in every aspect of our lives. Her words were burned into my being, "Of course you can see magic", she said. "Not only that, you can feel it, smell it and it will bathe you gently with spiritual love. You can find magic in everything you do...you just have to be aware of it. And that is your task - to find the magic in all aspects of life and in everything you do. When you can do that, you will never be sad, never be lonely, and never be fearful of living alone."

Wow...that was something I had a lot of problems with in my earlier life....being alone. I wasn't happy when I wasn't in a relationship. I can remember having boyfriends around long after the relationship was due to end – only because I didn't want to face the day alone. I find this very thing is a huge issue for human beings - especially women. We tend to need someone around to adore us. But after living on the mountain with only wild animals, I had found that living without another human being brings a sense of peace that cannot be found in cohabitation. It's not just that you can do whatever you want...eat what you want, etc. - it's an internal strength that is drawn from knowing you can take care of yourself – no matter what comes your way.

So how do we find magic in everything we do? Good question. Truly...there is magic in every single aspect of our life if we are aware. How many times have you heard that awareness is the key to spiritual realization? But when you press the issue and ask how one becomes aware, few people can give you a clue. To me, awareness is being in the moment and seeing what's right in front of us at this very moment. We aren't wrapped up in the past or worried about the future. We are just "HERE at this very second ". If we can remain in the "HERE at this moment", there are few issues to deal with. In most cases, the pain and suffering of one moment in time is relatively small. It's when we dwell on the heartaches we experienced in the past or worry about the future and what we will encounter that we get wrapped around the axel. Don't get attached to the things that make you happy and the things that upset you. Remember everything changes. See things for what they are – naked....without any spice.

I have a friend who is a master at adding spice where it doesn't need to be...she will give you every reason why things are happening...although she has no idea as to whether her reasons are accurate or not. She just honestly makes things up as she goes and professes that "she is sure she is right about the why". All she does is make up the most elaborate stories...which affect her day in and day out. That IS NOT Awareness.

Since the day my spiritual guide gave me the task to see the magic in everything, I seriously proceeded to do as she recommended. I learned something very important: Magic is only there when we interact with it...when we appreciate it and become part of it. And...then we have the most amazing, blissful experience. It's so worth it to attempt to live as a sage even if we aren't one yet. You know what they say, "fake it until you make it" and in spiritual practice, that is very valid. So rather than putting emotional spice on everyday issues, we can see the magic in all life by simply seeing things as they are....that's good enough.

As I shared before, trees are the essence of magic and, therefore, they help human beings in more ways than providing us with oxygen to breathe. They have an amazing ability to detoxify and nurture. Even the Buddha himself chose to become enlightened under a Bodhi Tree. Was it just a coincidence that he chose that tree...I don't think so. The tree gave him a magical advantage which assisted him in his quest for enlightenment. We tend to take trees and all of nature for granted. That's one reason why the world is in such trouble right now - because we humans destroy nature without a second thought. We use nature and abuse it - all the while not realizing that this will destroy us in the end if we don't change our view. We all know this but we continually ignore it. The rain forests are diminishing - which means the oxygen on this planet is diminishing. Do we see a problem here? Even if we choose a totally selfish view, what will happen to us when the oxygen level no longer sustains life on earth? Where did we feel we got the right...and the audacity to kill and use other beings for our own benefit? Nature is a huge collection of living beings - all unique and amazing. Even the smallest ant values its life just as much as we value ours.

Well, if there are people who don't even believe in global warming, then I guess they wouldn't believe in the detoxifying properties of trees and the importance of co-existing on this planet peacefully with all of nature. Everyone is free to have an opinion. To me, trees and all of nature can find a way to exist together without endangering one another. Nature is unconditional. But...are we?

Nature is the basis for Free the Mind – involving grass, trees, animals, birds...etc. Encountering nature and experiencing how its different parts interact perfectly with one another is the most beautiful thing to witness. You can learn all you need to know about Freeing the Mind by observing animals and birds in the dance of coexistence. These beings have far less attachments than we humans. Their only desires are food and sleep....and their primal nature pushes them to procreate. How many desires do we humans have? THAT would be a very long list.

We can learn something very valuable from the animals: The less desire one has, the less suffering one experiences. Letting go of some of our desires is extremely positive and will release a huge burden - allowing us to be much happier....and able to see the magic in life around us.

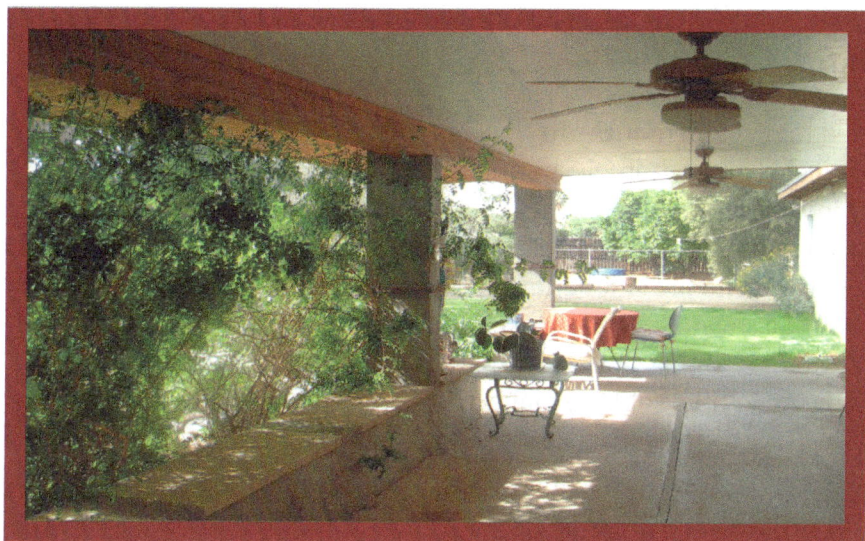

My Back Yard & its Inhabitants

BACK TO SCOTTSDALE TO LICK MY WOUNDS

For the last two and a half years I had been living in a heavenly place. My dream location: On the mountain with pine trees lining the ridge; wild animals meandering into my yard every day; and lots of quietude (at least most of the time). The air was clean and crisp - not at all like the brown haze that settled over the city of Scottsdale. So...I asked myself why-oh-why are you moving back to Scottsdale. The answer was to find another job after being laid off in November.

Well... plainly, the job search was not fruitful. So many thoughts ran through my mind - Would I ever find another job? How would I go into an office to work again after working from my home for so long? Did I want to work for a corporation again after being used and abused by them my whole career?

I tried for several months to find work but no luck. What would I do? Would I become a homeless person? Finally, I realized that I had many administrative and technical skills and perhaps I should just start my own business - which is what I did. I worked as a Virtual Assistant which is a person who provides administrative services from their own home. Soon I had several clients who kept me very busy. The virtual assistant work suited me just fine because that meant I could live anywhere I wanted and still be able to make a living. My back porch was my office. This wasn't the high-paying corporate job I was used to but it paid the bills, I was my own boss, and no one could lay me off....ever again.

I was pretty happy there in my house for a while - mostly because of Spencer but the noise and congestion of the city was too much to take and the mountains kept calling me back - loud and clear. So...there was nothing to stop me - Merlin and I weren't reconciling and there was nothing to keep me in Scottsdale. So I put my house up for rent again. On July 1, 2018 the new tenants took over and I was homeless – again. But....I was on a new journey and was very excited about where I would end up.

I headed towards northern Arizona. I thought it would be easier for me to keep an eye on my home if I was only a couple hours away. Places like Payson, Strawberry and Alpine were all beautiful with big tall trees but none of them felt right.... so I kept moving.

The thought occurred to me that I never really journeyed through western New Mexico so I set out for that trip and made my way from the southwestern corner of New Mexico all the way to Cortez, Colorado. New Mexico is beautiful in some places but the houses tend to be very run down and even the little towns in Arizona like Holbrook and Winslow just seemed depressed to me. The best thing about traveling through New Mexico is the wildlife and I saw plenty of it. I saw lots and lots of mule deer and elk...even 2 baby elk which I've not seen in the wild. They were so cute. I saw a couple of jack rabbits, skunks, and a fox. All great sightings for me.

I was driving through an area that I call "The Badlands of Colorado" and was nearing Cortez when I noticed some cloud formations in the sky over the mountains of Cortez. Was I really seeing this? The clouds had formed in the shape of a dragon – as clearly as if there was a picture in front of my eyes. As a child, I used to lay on my back in the grass and gaze up at the sky and would sometimes see figures that resembled something familiar but it only took a few seconds for the formation to distort because the clouds were constantly moving.

Interestingly enough, this dragon cloud formation didn't distort so I pulled over to the side of the road and watched for 10 minutes. The formation grew longer but the shape remained. The cloud formation was recognizable for about 15 minutes and then vanished as I entered Cortez. I had been through Cortez a couple of times during trips from Pagosa Springs back to Scottsdale but I never gave much thought to living there. For this journey I had planned on going directly to Pagosa Springs from Cortez but the dragon in the sky caused me to wonder whether my plan was going to be circumvented by someone in the ethereal realm. Was it an auspicious sign that I should live in this area? I wasn't sure but I realized I should explore the possibility. Maybe this dragon was pointing me to something amazing.

It was the July 4th weekend and Cortez was packed with tourists. Not one reasonably priced motel had a vacancy and the price to tent camp was $50 a night. I think not! I remembered a little place only 10 miles away from Cortez called Dolores, Colorado that was cute and quaint. Maybe there was a room for me there.

Dolores hadn't changed a bit since I last visited. In fact, it probably hasn't changed in the last 50 years. It is cute and rural...down-home folks ....and I liked it. I had considered it as a homestead back in 2014 when I was first looking for a place to live in Colorado. At the time, I was concerned that it was too small and that I may become too lonely in the winter time when I would be mostly staying inside. But things have changed in the last couple of years. My love of nature and wildlife had outgrown my desire for the company of human beings.

I decided to stay the night in Dolores if I could find a room – especially since the temperature was in the mid 90s and my computer, food and supplements would suffer if I left them in the car in that heat. I stopped at an interesting little motel called the Outpost that offered motel rooms as well as camping sites. I asked if there were any vacancies and the man behind the counter told me he had just checked in a wedding party and he had no vacancies at all – no motel rooms or camping sites. I couldn't believe it! Why in the world would I think there would be a motel room available in some of the most beautiful areas of Colorado on July 4th weekend? I was tired and wanted to rest and frustration was setting in. Before I knew it I was asking the motel owner if he knew of anyone who had a house for rent and to my surprise he quickly said, "Yes….I have a house for rent just outside of town". He told me that currently someone had rented the house for the week and I should come back on Monday morning to speak with his wife and at that time I could see the house.

This was possibly really good news and today was Saturday so I had only a day and a half to wait. I headed for Pagosa Springs which was about 2 hours from Dolores and the drive would be beautiful. As I drove through the mountain passes, I was in awe of the majestic pines that lined the ridge. All of a sudden, the trees started to sparkle as they did on my visit to Tara Mandala. I could hear them welcoming me back. They told me how happy they were that I had returned and they were looking forward to my teachings. My teachings?. Why were they telling me they were looking forward to my teachings? I had only begun to teach Free the Mind. Was I going to be teaching more? Sure sounded like it. All the way from Durango to Pagosa Springs the trees greeted me. It was awesome and it was a little weird…all wrapped up together.

I wondered how I would feel to enter Pagosa Springs again. I only had a couple of friends there but I thought it would be great to see them. Unfortunately, it was a holiday and I hadn't called ahead to give them a heads up. So, maybe at that point it was more important for me to go incognito than to reunite with friends.

Pagosa would be packed. I was sure of it. So I was in no hurry to get into the mess. I decided to stop by the house I had previously rented on the mountain. Seeing it brought back memories of Sunny and our amazing life together on that beautiful mountain. I stopped briefly by the side of the road to say hello to the trees and to see if I could catch a glimpse of Clark or Uhtred. But the first thing I saw in the yard was a big dog so I knew the deer were long gone from this house. How things had changed and made me a bit sad. But I reminded myself that things change - which is how the impermanent, material world works. There is only one thing that doesn't change and that is the pure essence of the Enlightened mind. That never never never changes and is the only thing real and permanent in our existence.

As I took in the beauty of the area, I thought of my heart friend, Clark and how much I loved him. Even if I didn't see him, I thought he would know that I was there. I stood and greeted the trees and tried to connect with Clark but was unable to. My Spiritual Guide then told me that he had passed away of natural causes during the winter. Well...I don't know what that meant. How does a deer die of "natural causes"? But I knew this was her way of side-stepping the whole subject so I shed a tear for him and knew I will always hold him dear to my heart. Thank you, Clark, for being my friend.

Soon I entered Pagosa Springs and it was bursting at the seams...as I had thought. I found a little motel room downtown – which I knew would be the most affordable. As I made my way to my motel room, a really cute cat stood between me and my door and he wasn't moving until I patted him. How could I not think of Sunny again? Lots of memories flooded back about my life in Pagosa Springs. Was this a good thing....or a bad thing to be back in Pagosa? Or was it just the way it was to be?

Even though I was alone in my motel room, I felt the hysteria of the crowd of tourists walking through town, bathing in the hot springs, tubing down the creek and walking through the small carnival. I realized I loved Pagosa Springs when I lived there because I lived outside of town and away from the hustle and bustle. I NEVER went near town on a holiday.

The next day I couldn't wait to get out of Pagosa Springs. I thought it would be good to go back to Cortez (which was a short distance to Dolores) and stay one more night...and then check on the availability of the house in Dolores on Monday morning. FINALLY, Monday had arrived. I chuckled to myself that this was the first time I was excited about a Monday morning. I started back to the Outpost Motel to take a look at the house for rent.

The whole way to Dolores, I was crossing my fingers that this house would work out...I was just not in the mood to live in motels until I found a house and there were absolutely no rental houses in Pagosa Springs at the time - at least not in a mountain setting.

I walked into the door of the Outpost and asked for "Ginger" and the lady at the desk said cheerfully, "That's me!" I liked her as soon as I laid eyes on her. She was like a sister I had just reunited with and she took me to the house that morning. As we entered the driveway, I saw two beautiful houses with two ponds at the lower end. As I walked down to take a closer look at the ponds, I was surprised and delighted to see a large bronze statue of a dragon. A dragon? Was the cloud formation in Cortez as I entered the town a message that I should rent the house with the dragon at the pond? I think so! This was a message that I needed to pay attention to. What are the odds of seeing a dragon cloud formation as I drove into Cortez and now here is a bronze statue of a dragon? Coincidence? I think not! The message came through loud and clear and I liked the setting of the house very much. Two ponds would bring in lots of wildlife and there was a creek below the ponds. There were lots of trees and a large yard....a beautiful setting. The only problem was that it was pretty close to the house Ginger also owned and lived in during the weekend when she wasn't taking care of the motel. It was too close for my taste but my Spiritual Guide told me that this is where I should stay...for now. She further explained that there were spiritual reasons for me to be here in this place at this time so I agreed and moved my belongings into the house that very day.

Dolores Greenery

ENDING UP IN DOLORES

Although Colorado consists of mountains, lakes, and streams, most of it is considered "high desert" in much of the state - which means it is fairly dry in nature. Coming from Scottsdale, Arizona (the Sonoran Desert), it was quite a change from anywhere I lived. I grew up in Central Pennsylvania which is very humid and green. Then there was a drastic change of terrain when I moved to Scottsdale...and then to Colorado which was different still.

Dolores was unique. It was located in a valley between mountain ranges and it was much wetter than the other parts of Colorado I've journeyed to. The yard was green and the ponds were filled with beautiful fish who loved to breach the surface of the pond in the morning when they were full of zest and vigor. I also watched as the kingfishers swooped down for their breakfast. The area was so alive with wildlife and so I made lots of friends. There were a couple of deer, ravens, magpies, beavers, an otter, fish and....many many mice who lived in the house. After my amazing experience with Clark (the deer) in Pagosa Springs, I expected that I would have the same loving deer friends here in Dolores but not the case. In fact, they wouldn't get within 50 yards of me unless I was sitting still on the porch as they walked by. Interesting how different areas bring forth different opportunities for wild friends.

Now...for the mice. Oh, they are so cute but many many many in number. When I saw my first mouse, I had a ridiculous thought....that he was the only one. I thought it wouldn't be bad to have some company in the house so I put out peanuts for him. He always ate them all.

One morning I came to the kitchen sink and noticed that he had taken many bites out of two peaches that were sitting on my window sill. He had also started gnawing on a sweet potato... I was happy to share but couldn't he have just eaten ONE of the peaches instead of taking several bites out of both? How rude! I started seeing a lot of mouse droppings and thought I better get some humane mouse traps. There could be more than one and I really wasn't interested in raising mice...although I love them as I do all living beings.

I soon realized the cruel mentality of Dolores. I had been to all the stores in town to find humane traps so I could escort those little guys out of the house rather than kill them with other kinds of snap traps. I even went to Cortez to find some live traps...with no luck. I finally ended up ordering online and 3 traps arrived in the mail so I set them in the evening.

To my surprise, all three traps were inhabited when I awoke the next morning. Hmmmm. I guess there was more than just one little guy. I released the cute little ones down at the pond but soon found out that they successfully found their way home and I had to begin taking them much farther away. I continued this practice the entire year I lived in Dolores. There was a whole colony of mice - adults and babies living very happily and comfortably in the house.

I spent so much energy trying to catch those little guys. Some of the babies were so small they wouldn't even trip the trap when they went in to grab a peanut. These mice were called "kangaroo mice" and they jumped like the dickens. Finally, the babies grew big enough to trip the door of the trap closed and I was able to relocate most of them. Still, I don't think I got them all...still a work in progress.

The reason I note this experience here is that just like the experience I had with the African bees, it would be very easy to just poison or use snap traps to kill the mice instead of going through the effort to capture and release them. But hurting them would not be easier for me. I would be heartbroken that they were hurt and disgusted with myself for taking that path.

In general, human beings tend to become disgusted with any animal that causes them irritation. The "just get rid of them" attitude reigns supreme in our culture. If you have a bee nest, call the exterminator. If you have rats in the garage, call the exterminator. If you have birds who make a mess on your patio, kill them.

I wonder where in the world did we get the attitude that the whole world is there to serve us and if anyone causes us any inconvenience, we should eliminate them. Where did we get the attitude that we have supreme power over all resources in this world and all the plants and animals who inhabit it. It's pretty obvious now that the planet is in a dismal state of decay. We have only ourselves to thank for global warming, cutting down the rainforests, and polluting the oceans. Now...who are the annoyances?

Well....it's a beautiful, cool morning in August - that doesn't happen much in Arizona...but it DOES happen in Colorado. Hurray!! I finally made it back to Colorado. I've been here for about a month and a half and it's wonderful. This morning I'm sipping my coffee by the pond as I normally do in the morning and feeling very much at peace. Thinking back on the last month, I realized it was difficult to get here. It felt like someone or something was trying to keep me in Arizona. I knew in my heart that I was to be back in Colorado somewhere even though I was very sure I would miss my friends in Scottsdale....especially Spencer. Saying goodbye to him for the third time was brutal.

As I relaxed with my coffee I realized "I'm sitting on my back porch in Dolores, Colorado and it's such a fine sight to see." Thank you Jimmy Buffet! The property is wooded but not deeply wooded so the sun sparkles through the green leaves of the willow trees and warms the heart and the soul.

As I mentioned, there are two ponds on the property and a small creek runs through which nourishes the land and provides a water source to draw the animals in so I can observe and make friends with them. Forest fires are currently raging in Colorado and my heart bled for the innocent animals and greenery who are dying as a result. Perhaps I'm here to help with that? I would obviously do whatever I could to help so I asked my Spiritual Guide what action I was to take.

"What do you think?", she replied. "If I knew, I wouldn't have asked you", I replied. "Ask them to bring the rain", she said...a bit annoyed.

I had no idea how to request rain from "Them" but I went out into the yard, raised my hands to the sky and asked for "Them" to bring the rain. I had no idea what I was doing.

The next couple of days went by and it was as dry as ever. I requested again....no rain. Finally I got a bit irritated and asked "Them" why they wouldn't answer my request...not for myself but for the flora and fauna of the land. I obviously wasn't getting anywhere.

I was frustrated but tried again and got an answer...not one I relished but still, an answer. I heard a wrathful voice say, "Why should we help you...you're a real pain." I was happy now because at least I got a response, although I wasn't sure if this response came from "Them" or from my own mind and I was now having a conversation with myself.

I asked this being to identify herself and she said she was a Naga being and I was starting to irritate her. She informed me that she and others like her inhabited the lakes and streams. They could bring the rain but they wondered why I was requesting and how arrogant I was to think they would do as I asked.

The Nagas insulted and provoked me for quite some time but I hung in there for the sake of beings who were suffering. After much conversation and humbling on my part, they informed me they would satisfy my request and bring the rains to quench the thirst of the land. In the end, I believe they were just trying to get my attention because they seemed to have a history with me but I have few memories of my past lives. They knew me well enough to dangle in front of me the one thing that would get a rise out of me.....watching wildlife and the flora of the land suffer.

Conversing with beings from a realm most of us have never heard of sounds a little New Agie....doesn't it? At first I thought so too but then I realized it was all about expanding one's mind to understand that it is arrogant and imperialistic for me to believe that the only beings who exist in this universe are those I can see and hear. The Nagas live alongside humans and we have no knowledge of their existence. A lack of awareness? Maybe. But maybe we just never realized we can see them. Maybe this is an error in perception because our culture teaches us that animals, birds, fish,insects and ourselves are the only beings that inhabit the earth. But...that's not true.

I thought back to my early teachings of Free the Mind in Scottsdale and Pagosa Springs when I invited all beings - whether they be animals, humans, or unseen beings to my teachings. I was amazed at the animals who stopped by as well as other beings who I sensed but couldn't see. Where was I going with this? Only time will tell but with the introduction to the Nagas, I had a feeling that my mind was about to expand even more. But...who was I to consider that I had the spiritual essence strong enough to bring the rain? Oh....but then I didn't have to bring the rain. I just had to convince the Nagas to bring the rain.

Contemplating all of this reminded me of my visit to Dolores back in 2014 when I began my first journey to find a house on the mountain. The road that goes through Dolores and continues up over the mountain leads to Telluride, CO – a famous skiing location. I decided to take the journey to the top of the mountain to see Telluride because my friend Dorje once visited the town and he thought it was amazingly beautiful. The longer I drove towards Telluride, the blacker the clouds became and the wind whipped around my car like a woman scorned. Soon it felt like the mountain would swallow me up if I didn't turn around and go back. This mountain was actually kicking me out and so I retreated. What did I do to anger this mountain? I had no idea but I did know I wasn't interested in battling a mountain....I'm pretty sure I would lose.

Obviously, at the present moment, this same mountain welcomed me to Dolores with open arms. I wondered again about my purpose here. Was there any purpose at all? Am I to somehow help with the fires or did it just happen this way? These questions were something to contemplate but not dwell on.

The next day it rained and it rained every day after that....for weeks. Soon the fires had been reduced and the land was recuperating. Was this a coincidence? Hmmmm. After all...it wasn't me that brought the rain. The Nagas had simply answered my sincere request to nurture the land. That's pure altruism - we help one another.

Sitting on a porch looking out at the beautiful trees, I wonder if life could get any better. The robins had already come to welcome me and hummingbirds whisked by to drink the nectar I offered them. I really miss Spencer and his clan so much but my journey brought me here and I sure hope he understands.

My Favorite Pond

Notice the Dragons on the Other Side of the Pond

Talking (not sleeping) with the Fisheys

My days were simple in Dolores. The office for my work was as it was in Scottsdale - out on the back porch so I could see any wildlife that came into my field of vision. But the mornings began with a cup of coffee by the pond. I never knew who I would meet down there. I was eager to meet anyone who came by, watch the kingfishers swooping in for their breakfast and experience the fish breaching the surface of the pond.

The ponds on the property were side by side but very unique. One had darker water that was fed from an underground spring and the other was fed by the creek that ran next to it. I preferred the small dark one. It was abundant with life and so many fish. I would sit beside its still waters for hours enjoying the peace and the animal beings who visited the pond. There were otters, beavers, eagles, an assortment of ducks, egrets and king fishers.

One morning during my coffee by the pond, one of the fish breached the water so beautifully that he looked like a tiny porpoise showing off. Instinctively, I called out, "Whoo Hoo look at that magnificent jumper...he can really jump!" It's a good thing I was alone at the pond or the neighbors would have thought I lost it. As soon as I called out, another jumped and another. The more I Woo Hoo'd, the more they jumped. Was this my imagination or did the fish like hearing me cheer for them? From that point on, this was our morning ritual. They would jump and I would cheer. It was so much fun.

I never tried to verbally communicate with fish because fishermen have told me they don't like noise so you have to be very quiet when fishing. Maybe fish aren't afraid of noise but, instead, it's the sharp hook on the other side of a tasty morsel they fear. Regardless....these fish liked the sound of my voice and they played with me every morning. It was a beautiful time. I decided that if I was giving a teaching on Free the Mind, I should do it by the pond and invite the fish to attend. After all...is inviting the fish to a teaching any more unusual than cheering them to jump in the mornings? They seemed to like me and I liked them so...why not? All beings have the essence of the Buddha Nature within them - it's that spark that never changes and holds the possibility for enlightenment. Who was I to decide another being's fate? I would invite ALL beings to attend and those who chose to show up were the ones who chose to progress on their spiritual path. Free the Mind was for everyone!

I hadn't given a teaching in a while - ever since Pagosa Springs and even during those two years, I had only given a handful of sessions. Looking back at my time in Pagosa revealed a time of great suffering - and great growth. I've heard that times of pain and heartache really bring forth amazing songs from great performers. The same was true for me. The first year in Pagosa was one of the worst in my life. I was first struggling with my relationship with Merlin and then our break up; then the crushing death of Sunny...not to mention losing my job and having to reinvent myself. All of these life changes took a toll on me and catapulted me to another level of insight, wisdom and desire to share with others so that they would also reach new levels. And...who was able to help me mend my heart? A little furry wild cat named Sunny who gave me strength to pick up the pieces of my heart and mend it back together with his undying love for me. Unconditional love is a precious gift animals give to humans. And...we humans are not always as loyal to them as they are to us.

All of these experiences brought about amazing insights for me...after a lot of introspection and continual training from my Spiritual Guide. This was a time of great pain and great spiritual growth and so the unfolding of Free the Mind began to bubble up inside of me and details were revealed.

All the turmoil and growth during this time brought forth introspection and a new outlook on my part. I felt a heightened sense of strength and fortitude - and a faith in myself that I never quite had before. I always knew my inner perseverance was one of my most positive attributes but now all the fluff was gone. And in its place was introspection, contentment and peace. In other words...wisdom. It took alot of internal work before I was capable of teaching Free the Mind effectively. Now, I have come out the other side of pain and suffering into the new light of helping others progress along their spiritual path.

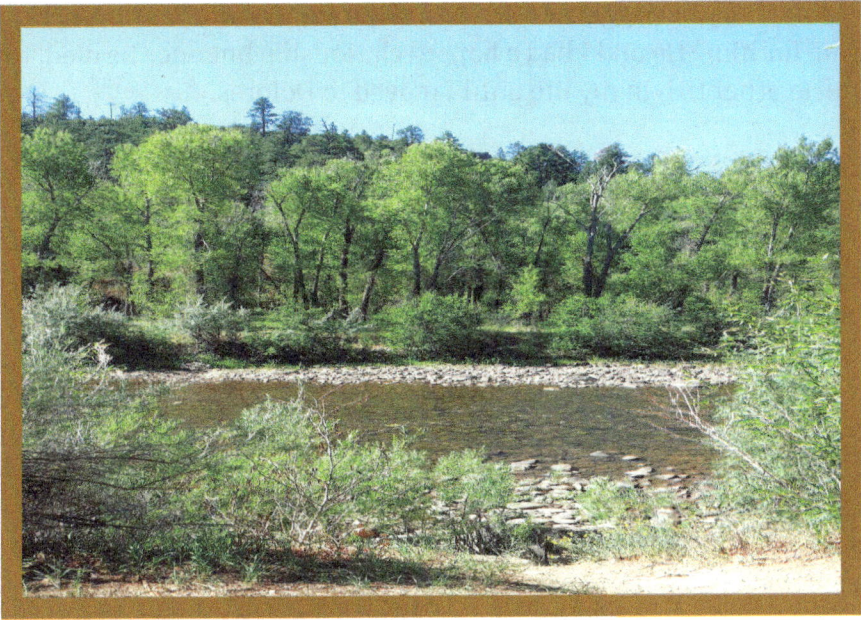

Creek Behind the House

THE TEACHINGS BEGIN

When I was a kid, I loved my aquarium of freshwater fish. I had live plants to adorn the environment and also to nourish the fish themselves. But since I moved out of my family home in the farm country in Central Pennsylvania, I haven't really encountered many fish.

Reggie was an exception. Reggie was a Chinese Fighting fish my daughter talked me into buying because she felt I was lonely and needed a pet to take care of. I couldn't convince her that I was not lonely but since I appreciated that she was looking out for me, I went to the pet store and bought Reggie and all the paraphernalia that went along with caring for him. He and I had a happy relationship but once he died, there were no other fish in my life until I moved to Dolores.

The first class of Free the Mind - Dolores was a couple days away and I hadn't taught in quite a while. In fact, the information I was receiving from my Guide was coming so fast that I felt overwhelmed. I had NEVER taught this level of Free the Mind. It had developed, matured and was much more powerful and focused than when I began teaching five years ago. My realizations were more pervasive and my understanding had deepened. There was no space for stroking and placating students. This teaching was not for the faint of heart. There were no "feel good" meditations or joyous chanting.... only getting down to work. "Do you want to become enlightened...or not?" was my mantra and those students who persevered would reap the benefits. But the outline of the class, who would attend, where it would be given and how long it would be offered were all unknowns to me. Only one being had the answer to those questions....my Spiritual Guide and she wasn't talkin'.

Two days before the first class I decided to rehearse to see how the teaching flowed. The weather was superb so I walked down to the pond with my notes and sat down to rehearse. A few minutes after I began doing a dry run of the class out loud I noticed that the fish started congregating near me – perhaps 5-7 at a time. They seemed to enjoy my voice even though I wasn't cheering them on for their jumps. I knew my decision to teach by the pond to involve the fish was a great idea. The teaching would be extended not only to the fish but also to the earth spirits. These unseen beings live in and nurture the trees and other flora of the land so they would also have the opportunity to hear the teaching by the pond. It was obvious that I wouldn't have any human students at this point. But ALL beings have the Buddha Nature and are capable of becoming enlightened. I would teach those who came to listen. They were the audience who were ready to hear Free the Mind and were ready to progress on the spiritual path. Sounds crazy? Not to me.

I did alot of teaching that summer in Dolores. Every Sunday would bring a teaching by the pond (when weather permitted). When rain blessed us, the large back porch was our refuge. From June to November the teachings progressed and it was a wonderful experience for me. Many different kinds of beings attended. What was interesting was that by the end of the teachings, they all sat together....intermingling.

Eagle Eye. Hard to believe...but it's true.

One friend I made while sitting at the pond was a baby golden eagle. He would call to me and I would return the call. I think this little guy got bored when his mother was off hunting so calling me was a fun activity. This relationship reminded me so much of Serena and the summer we spent together. Oh how I missed her.

One day I was sitting at the pond and I heard Percy (I felt that the eagle was a boy) calling to me in the weirdest eagle call I've ever heard. It sounded more like a melody than a predator's screech. I called back to him in that same melodic tone. He called back and then flew over my head and called to me again. He landed in the tree beside me and sat and watched me for a while – then back to his tree by the creek. His mother soon returned so the conversation stopped temporarily. But from that point on, he would call out to me every time he saw me. And let's be real – he saw me waaaay before I saw him. Even though he was considered a "juvenile" eagle, he looked to be full grown and if you haven't seen an eagle close up, you're missing something important. They are powerful and formidable and not a force to be messed with.

This beautiful interaction went on until the salmon began to run. That's when the "eagle convention" took place and the eagles came from miles around to feast. What a sight to see! One morning I counted over 30 eagles in two huge trees – some bald eagles, some goldens, and some eagles I couldn't identify. What a huge bundle of power sitting in those two trees. I'll never forget it.

After the salmon run, Percy and I would say good morning to one another but the weather had turned pretty brisk and I knew my time with him would soon come to an end. At that point he would fly further south for warmer weather.

I cherished every morning I had with the eagle and fish so even though it was a bit cold, I went to the pond with my coat, hat and gloves and, of course, my cup of coffee. One breezy morning I sat down to talk with Percy and I heard a sound that I hadn't heard before. Windchimes from the neighbor's house echoed through the canyon wall of the creek. It was a clear morning – unusually quiet – so the windchimes really pierced through the crisp morning air. The melody sounded familiar. Where had I heard that sound before?

Suddenly, I heard Percy calling to me in that same melodic tone and it registered. This was utterly amazing but Percy had been hearing the sound of those windchimes for months as he grew up and he was mimicking that sound in order to converse with me.

I sat there in awe and it took a couple minutes for me to digest what had happened and to really believe what I had experienced. A couple things I am sure of – Percy learned how to mimic a sound in order to communicate with a human. That skill shows conceptual processing and verbal communication. What intelligence!

Eleanor

YOU'RE SUCH A TURKEY

As I've stated earlier, in every place I've lived, I make many animal friends but there's always a species that is oh-so-special to me. There must be a past-life connection with those animals and birds who just walk or fly up to me and make friends with only minimal effort on my part. They always turn out to be the best friends a girl could want. Spencer and Serena from Scottsdale; Sunny and Clark from Pagosa Springs, and Percy, the Fisheys and Eleanor from Dolores.

One day in August I was working diligently at my Virtual Assistant job on the porch and I noticed a big bird enter my yard– one that I never saw in the wild before and one that was unmistakably a wild turkey. Very beautiful, very big and a little scary. I certainly wouldn't want a bird this big to decide she didn't like me.

I sat still and watched in silence and soon the being vanished into the wooded area. The next day, the turkey appeared again. This time I wasn't so shocked and she and I had a short conversation.

I had heard wild turkeys gobbling up on the ridge behind my house in Pagosa, but had never met one in person. The turkey seemed to be fully at ease with me. Knowing little about the species, it wasn't clear whether this bird was a male or female but after a bit of research, it became clear that she was an amazing female wild turkey – powerful and proud. I named her "Eleanor". At that moment, I recalled this is how most of my special animal relationships begin. A being wanders near me; I talk with him/her; they talk to me and we strike up a friendship. I was happy to meet someone I'd never met before and was looking forward to a beautiful relationship with a new friend.

It was my understanding that turkeys thrive in groups called rafters so it seemed strange that she was alone but, hey....I was alone too. Maybe we both enjoyed some solitude! She had her routine and several times a day she would pass the porch and we would say our salutations. When she saw me, she would primp, ruffle her feathers and flap her wings...as if to show off. Hmmmm...maybe she thought I was a male of the species.

Some afternoons she would actually bed down for a nap under the shade of the willow and pine trees in the yard. There she would rest while I continued my daily work. If she entered the yard when I was concentrating on a project and didn't look her way, she would make a soft tweeting sound similar to the sound of baby chicks. I enjoyed spending time with Eleanor and hoped she would hang out with me for a bit. We girls had to stick together!

Offering Food to the Turkeys

THE TURKEYS

My relationship with Eleanor extended all summer. We were two independent females taking pleasure in our "girlfriend" relationship. One day in early September Eleanor walked into the yard as she had done so often and then I spied another smaller female coming right towards her. The thought occurred to me that perhaps this was one of her family, a child, or someone she knew and I was happy to know Eleanor was no longer a lone turkey. When the two turkeys met in the middle of the yard, it was obvious that they were not familiar. They passed one another without much of a "how do you do."

Right after that incident, Eleanor stopped visiting and I hoped beyond all hope that she was alright. I didn't see her at all for weeks and then one day I was in town, walking along the river and saw a turkey on the other side of the creek. It sure looked like Eleanor but let's face it – I've only ever seen two turkeys up close in my life so I wasn't sure. I called to her and she looked like she recognized me but she was on the other side of the river and we each went our own way.

About a month after seeing the turkey by the creek, I was driving home after doing some errands and a group of turkeys flew across the road in front of my car only a short distance from my home. I thought that surely one of them had to be Eleanor. I was hoping she joined the group because my intuition told me she really didn't relish being alone. Although I missed seeing Eleanor during our daily visits, she needed to be with her own kind for protection and camaraderie.

A week later I was eating breakfast and couldn't believe my eyes: A group of 12 turkeys wandered around my backyard foraging for food. I stood in wonder of these giant birds. Since I had never met a turkey (either wild or tame) until meeting Eleanor, I had little understanding as to how they interacted with one another, how to tell males from females, or how they would behave around me. I watched as the clan casually ate bugs and grubs from the yard. They all looked pretty much alike except that there were a few larger than the others. From pictures of turkeys, I expected to see fan tails on the males but none had their plumes out. I asked myself, "Were they all females?" Getting to know these beings would be an entirely new experience for me and I was excited to learn more about them.

I walked out on the porch to see if I could talk with them and one came up to me right away. It was Eleanor! I was so very happy to see my friend and I wanted her friends to accept me so I ran inside and grabbed some peanuts to offer.

They all watched me offering food to Eleanor and stayed at a distance but they didn't run away. Suddenly, the males "plumed" and THEN I could definitely see the difference physically between male and female turkeys. The males' gobblers on their beaks also changed color from red to silver as they ruffled their feathers to make themselves look larger. WOW...I was in awe.

I didn't realize the males are not in full fan all the time. Of course, it would be very difficult to run or fly with their fans out...hee hee. As I got to know them, I witnessed that they fanned out when they wanted to challenge another for territory, for breeding rights, to prove who was in charge, or just to show off. The males pranced around displaying their wares for half an hour and then all 12 turkeys mosied on their way. I was so excited to make some friends – especially those I never had the pleasure to meet before.

I relished spending time with the turkeys and over the next months, they grew to love me (or the tasty morsels I offered them...hee hee) and their number grew from 12 to approximately 50. Soon Eleanor introduced me to her mate. I named him Zeus because he was a large, beautiful, powerful mature turkey and was a force to be reckoned with. He wasn't the leader of the flock but one of the leader's captains.

The turkey clan had a daily routine which began with bath time every morning down at the pond. They were adorable flapping around at the water's edge and it was obvious they took extreme pleasure in it.

Then it was time to go to Tara's Cafe just up over the hill and they all flocked to my backyard to enjoy some breakfast. Imagine feeding 50 turkeys! I became quite an expert at making popcorn and many times I had two popcorn poppers going at the same time. I also offered them bread and peanuts. It was amazing to walk among them while they enjoyed the food. I remember telling a friend of mine about my adventures with the turkey clan and he warned me to be careful. He went on to say that turkeys can be extremely mean and aggressive. Well...I never experienced any of that with them. I would walk right up to the big males as I offered the popcorn and they would just move away to let me pass. It was a totally loving relationship and we appreciated one another very much. They were hilarious at times and so interesting that I couldn't wait to see them in the morning and evening and sometimes if snow was in the air or there was fresh snow on the ground, they would just sit in the back yard or on the fence during the day and then go to bed from there.

Bedtime for the turkeys was very intriguing. These huge birds would actually sleep high in the cottonwood trees. I watched in amazement as they congregated and flew from one low branch to another higher branch until they were high in the trees. And each time they flew to a higher level, they made a honking sound. When I looked at the "turkey trees" in the evening, the birds were so high in the trees that all I could see were round dots on the branches where the turkeys rested.

It was a long winter with lots of snow and every time I saw the flakes floating from the sky, my heart went out to the turkeys. At times they had to wade through some really deep snow - up to their hips. I knew, however, that for most of them, this wasn't their first winter in Dolores, Colorado. The amount of popcorn I bought and prepared for them probably boosted the local economy but I was happy to offer it. They were intriguing beings and I enjoyed every moment of my relationship with them.

I was relieved when spring came and the weather wasn't so cold. The turkeys were really feeling their oats after several cold months. They were frisky and the males spent a lot of time sparring for mating rights.

One morning I heard quite a bit of commotion out in the yard so I went to the back porch to see what was transpiring with my friends. I could see a group of 6 turkeys walking together down toward the pond - making a lot of racket and stretching their necks up toward the sky. I watched in amazement as they chased a lone coyote away from the flock. Wow....those guys really WERE tough. Later that morning, a neighbor's dog wandered into the yard and they had already mobilized their protection group and were headed down to show the dog who was boss. I had to intervene to save the dog from injury because those turkeys had no problem protecting their home.

One day my landlord had come to spend the weekend in his country home and the turkeys took part in their normal routine - bath by the pond and breakfast at Tara's. I knew he was an avid hunter and turkey hunting season (the most loathsome time of the year) was right around the corner. I am sure that if he walked out his door and shot a turkey, I would have taken off after him - like I did when the young boy shot a deer in his yard in Pagosa.

So...I started down to the pond to try to avoid a casualty and an altercation. My plan was to gently usher the turkeys into the woods and away from the yard - to protect them. When I started to approach the pond, Eleanor saw me coming and headed straight towards me with two other smaller turkeys by her side. When we approached each other, Eleanor and her two companions stopped about 6 feet from me and we had a short talk. Soon the rest of the flock were gathering and approaching me. Eleanor then meandered around me and went about her business and all the turkeys came toward me and split into two groups – with a steady stream of turkeys passing me on both sides and me standing in the middle. It was one of the most heart-warming moments I've had with wild animals. They weren't afraid of me in any way but just going about their business and peacefully greeting me. The landlord never came out of the house (thankfully) so there wasn't an altercation.

A week later I stopped at the landlord's place of business to pay my monthly rent and he smiled at me and said, "Ya know, Tara...I saw the turkeys with you the other day. I never saw anything like that in my life. It was amazing....I'm gonna call you the turkey whisperer. That was a wonderful compliment and I held that in my heart. As the weeks went by, I became closer and closer to my flock and I realized that they were totally in charge. I offered food to them morning and night and would joyfully walk among them. I would rise early in the morning to prepare the food and spend time with them. If I dared to oversleep, they would call out to me until I stirred - no mistake who was in charge of this relationship. Eleanor stayed close to me and followed behind me when I walked through the flock offering food. I could claim that she loved me so much that she followed me around, but the truth is that I tended to drop food as I walked and she intelligently was happy to clean up behind me.

Soon hunting season was approaching and I didn't want to provide hunters with an easy way to kill lots of turkeys in a big group so I ceased the food offering. I wanted my friends to head for the hills for safety. I know I had saved some lives during the extremely cold and snowy winter, but now it was spring and they could find lots of food for themselves. They passed by for a week or two but then the mountain called them and they traveled up to higher elevations. I will always remember my 50 turkey friends in Dolores, Colorado and I cherish their friendship.

What I learned from the Turkeys: Bravery on behalf of the group and altruism for one's fellow beings.

Male Turkeys in All Their Glory

BRAVERY

As I studied the wild turkeys closely, I realized they symbolized the epitome of altruism and bravery. They actually embodied the philosophy of the Three Musketeers - "One for all and all for one." On cold winter days, when the weather was extra frigid, I witnessed male turkeys chasing after hens who were laying too long in the snow. That practice of keeping their flock moving wasn't done on warmer days. I reasoned that it is important to keep the blood moving when it's frigid and it may be dangerous to sit still too long in the cold snow - they could freeze. They protect their own. Many times, as I watched them stand up for one another, I contemplated what it meant to be brave in the human realm. Going off to war to protect one's country, standing up for those who cannot speak for themselves, and offering food to those who are hungry all warm my heart when I see those heroes watching the backs of others.

It is honorable to assist others, however, before we can take care of others, we need to first take care of ourselves - to feel confident in our abilities and our path. We can only effectively help others when we are brave spiritually. When we are willing to work hard to progress along the spiritual path and feel the path welling up inside of us, ONLY THEN can we effectively extend our help to others.

I don't like cities but there was one thing I loved about Scottsdale - a Starbucks right down the street. One morning I was sitting in the drive-thru line when I saw a bumper sticker on the fender of the car ahead of me that said, "B BRAVE!" The line was moving but the person in the "brave" car just sat there - obviously distracted. The driver was staring straight ahead, lost in her thoughts or confusion – not sure which. Normally, I would just brush the incident off but today it struck me that our society really stresses how important it is to be "brave" – but what exactly does our society consider a brave act? This woman in front of me obviously had a need to put that particular bumper sticker on her car. No matter what the reason, at this very moment she was totally UNAWARE of who she was and what she was doing.

It struck me that one of the major human diseases in our society is not that we are cowards, but that we are totally unaware. We hear from the yoga, spiritual, or meditative community of the importance of awareness but how well is this word explained. Do we really know what it means to be aware? Without awareness, we have no hope of progressing spiritually so it's important to be clear.

In a nutshell, awareness is being awake - observing and experiencing our internal world as well as the external. In the final analysis, both internal and external are the same. If we are sentient beings, our society and our reaction to society's rules have created who we are. Our culture molds and controls us from the moment we come into this world until the time we leave it. The rules keep us in place and keep us tied to the physical world. Awareness of who we are and why we are here on this planet is crucial to taking the first step to breaking those chains that bind us...and to take the first step upon the spiritual path.

Sit for a few minutes and embrace the atrocities that are taking place right now against every species on the planet. Sadly, you'll come to the realization that humankind is at the core of all of these cruelties against nature and even to ourselves. If you can find yourself in the place of truly feeling what we earthlings have knowingly and unknowingly done to the planet, you will hang your head and cry. I know I did. That's why it is important that someone say these words out loud. That way we can all own up to what we have done and we can begin to heal ourselves and our planet. We as a species have collectively created the issues. The good news is that if we accept accountability for the problems, we can heal them – one day at a time.

A very simple way to begin is to be kind to animals,birds, and nature in general. They are so easy to please. They really don't want much – just some food and water and they're happy. They will never harm you or hate you but those little guys may steal from you a bit. The animal kingdom doesn't have a "do not steal" rule.

No matter where I live, there is a bowl of peanuts on the kitchen counter by my back door. It's convenient for offering a treat to my chipmunk friends who run up the outside of the kitchen window and sit on the screen waiting for a tasty morsel. The birds are fans of peanuts too as are the squirrels and even the deer. Of course, I've already revealed that I normally leave my back door open. The other day I was working in my office when I heard rattling in the peanut bowl. I walked out to see the peanuts strewn all over the floor and the bowl was in the sink. Who did it? Let's see...there is a long list of possible culprits and every one of them makes me chuckle. Could it have been the thrashers (birds) or the cactus wren? Hmmmm...this was a pretty big job - must have been the squirrels. The perpetrator was gone, of course, since the sound of the bowl crashing into the sink probably scared the little one.

I walked out onto the back porch but no one would fess up. I could have been angry because I had a mess on the floor but that didn't occur to me because I was honored that this being felt comfortable enough to enter my kitchen and help himself. We encourage human guests to make themselves at home when they visit so why not extend the same courtesy to animal friends? Animals and birds can bring us joy, happiness and contentment. They are funny and smart and they want to get to know us.

I've experienced birds fly into my kitchen and eat mac & cheese from my stove – so I learned to keep the pan covered. I love to eat lunch and dinner on the back porch so I took my plate of spaghetti out to the table at noon and realized I forgot a fork. Big mistake. By the time I got the fork and came back out to the table, a bird was prancing around my spaghetti. I have never laughed harder in my life, although I really had a strong desire for spaghetti that night. Oh well, the joy I felt warmed my heart when I realized this bird felt totally comfortable taking what he thought was being offered to him. I've had squirrels run into my office through the back door and refuse to leave until I produced a peanut and I've had adorable ground squirrels take a peanut from my hand only to hide it in my sock drawer. Did this little guy hide the peanut as an offering to me or did she plan to come back later and claim it? Not sure. But all my animal and bird friends are totally enjoyable to watch and interact with.

As you can imagine, my backyard is my sanctuary. Anyone who enters this sacred place, is in awe. I haven't spent thousands of dollars on landscaping and fountains. Nothing fancy. I just allowed the plant kingdom to do what it wanted. It's plush and green and is a wonderland. I planted an organic vegetable garden and a few herbs but mostly I allowed the native plants and weeds to flourish. Rather than chopping down "weeds", I watched them grow and they became part of a beautiful Garden of Eden.

The same is true for the birds and animals that I welcome into my world. They are accepted for who they are and they seem to enjoy spending time with me - just as I do with them. We all work together to create a sanctuary that we call home. That's why my friends enter the kitchen and help themselves - they feel comfortable and entitled to do so because this is their home and we are family.

Try this yourself: Buy a hummingbird or a wild bird feeder and observe birds that will come to eat. You will get to know them and love them - just as they will get to know you. If you really want to experience joy, buy a bird bath and keep it filled with fresh water. There's nothing more enjoyable than watching birds bathe - they thoroughly enjoy it. And having a hummingbird buzzing your head is the most fascinating experience. As I've said, if you have the honor of holding one of these little fairies in your hands, you'll never forget it.

If you see rabbits in the yard, cut up an apple or carrot. They will appreciate it. Take time to sit outside and observe them. After they get used to seeing you and realize you are the source of the food and water, they will call your yard home and be delighted to see you. Yes, there will be bird droppings and the rabbits and squirrels may eat some of your plants...but so what? They will bring you a chuckle when you're not feeling your normal chipper self.

When I really needed support, the birds and animals were always there for me. They are never too busy to chat for a while. Just watching the grackles gather around the bird bath and take turns splashing around in the water rejuvenates me. When I lived in Scottsdale, the love birds used to gather around the bird bath when the grackles came in for water games. Since a love bird's beak is rounded downward like that of a parrot, it's hard for them to throw water up in the air to bathe. Not a problem. The grackles were happy to oblige them and both species gathering together while the grackles provided a good splash for their lovebird friends was amazing for me to watch. Bath Sharing.

Animals and birds honor the pecking order and protocol they learned from their parents. My Mother told me that when she visited Africa some years ago she and her husband took a jeep trip through the Serengeti. She witnessed a mother wild pig tragically watching her baby die. The mother pig nudged it for an hour and tried to bring the baby back to life – but to no avail. She squealed and cried knowing that her baby had died. My Mother realized that animals feel the same pain - both physically and emotionally as we humans do. I wonder how we can ever convince ourselves that the death of her baby didn't cause that mother pig great despair? Human parents who lose babies may never fully recuperate from their loss so how can we be so cold as to believe these flesh and blood animals (like us) feel no emotional pain? Think about baby calves and sheep who are taken from their mothers very early in their lives to create lamb or veal chops?

It's time. It's time that we learn to share the earth with all beings - not just think of our own selfish endeavors. I hope the human race will be able to embrace and understand this concept. That's why I was motivated to write this book. Otherwise, I would just be wasting my time and effort – preaching to people who cannot hear. But I really believe we are ready to live harmoniously with all beings and when the mindset of the masses switches gears, the disasters that are plaguing the human race will subside. I have faith in us. When there is a disaster, we all work together. During the latest hurricanes, people helped each other and they also helped the animal kingdom. I read that people were rescuing manatees who were stranded in Florida as a result of the back current of the ocean. I applaud you all and I'm so proud.

Now it's time to contemplate deeper and realize that all we earthlings - whether we be animals, birds, plants, insects or humans - are in this together. We all have a path to walk and we can live harmoniously while we walk that path.

We humans want to be happy but at what cost? Would you choose "happiness" over your own spiritual advancement? I know I absolutely would not. Happiness is fleeting - one day we are happy about a relationship, a new job, or a new house and the next day we are hurt and unhappy because our life is not unfolding the way we want it to. Emotions are changeable because they are a part of the ego mind - which fluctuates constantly. Remember that we came to this world to learn - to realize who we truly are and taking a detour that gives us temporary happiness is not really the wise path.

Choosing the path that gives us space to learn is always the best choice or choosing to be alone for a while is an even better choice. My advice is not to settle for less than you deserve. Buddhist teachings proclaim that life is a pattern of hills and valleys and there is no way to avoid that unless we become enlightened. I believe that is true - we absolutely can CHOOSE to become enlightened.

I advise that you never make a choice because it is the easiest. Being challenged helps us grow and encourages us to aspire to a more lofty existence. Until we find a mirror who can show us who we are and help us grow, we will remain complacent. A spiritual journey has challenges and pitfalls but without them, we will never be free. My first Buddhist Teacher told me, "You can win the greatest battle or travel to the most exotic place, but you will never truly find peace until you have the courage to experience your own mind." We all have the spark of Enlightenment within us and we have an opportunity every moment of our lives to become Enlightened. The Mind is powerful - and encompasses the vast sea of the Pure Mind. The Buddha said, 'I am not who you think I am. YOU are who you think I am'".

It's All About Us

WHAT IT MEANS TO BE HUMAN

Have you ever asked yourself the question, "What does it mean to be human? Why am I not an animal or insect? Why am I human?

This may sound like a crazy question but I've asked myself that question from the time I was in my early 20s. For those of us who believe that we are born and reborn and live many, many lifetimes, we have learned that (according to Buddhism and other spiritual groups), we are reborn according to our "good" and "bad" deeds.....according to our karma.

Growing up as a Christian, I had more than one conflict with my church's Reverend. He threatened to kick me out of catechism class and told my father that I didn't "fit the mold". Not sure what mold he was referring to but I'm pretty sure he meant that I wasn't adopting the doctrines of the word of God "correctly" so, therefore, I wasn't a good Christian.

My father punished me because I was "giving the Pastor a hard time". Truthfully, all I was really doing was stating my beliefs and I guess because those beliefs were NOT in alignment with the doctrines of the church, I was a nuisance. Maybe I was. And...maybe I still am. I remember one conversation I had with this same Reverend after the tragic death of my brother - when he told me that (as I mentioned previously), the reason for my brother's death was that heaven "needed little angels." That was a pivotal point for me. I saw clearly that many of us hear statements like the one I heard at my brother's wake and rather than investigate the gist of the meanings, we simply repeat them - whether they make sense or not. Then others repeat them as well and no one really understands what is being said. These pass-it-on ideas are thoughtless and ignorant.

Depending on what religious regime we follow will depend on how much arrogance and vanity we exhibit. Some of us believe that we humans are just one of the many species that thrive here on our Mother Earth....and some of us believe we ARE the superior species and we deserve to reign over all other species on this earth. In fact, some believe animals and birds were put here to serve us. Oh yeah...I am truly on a roll when it comes to this.

We have to remember that the Bible and the Buddhist Sutras may have been taught by Enlightened beings but they were physically written down by people - from a human perspective. Any information we read about nature is also written from our human perspective. How can we judge the intelligence of another species through human eyes? It's extremely subjective.

I would bet animals and birds think we humans are not the smartest of beings. We are wasteful with food and throw perfectly good food away - which they will eat if they get hold of it. Animals and birds don't have a lot of ego. They will beg for food and take any crumbs we humans will toss their way.

We are so arrogant to think that all other beings in this world were put here to feed or entertain us. And that's only the more positive thoughts we have. Some of us feel we should regulate the numbers of animals on earth or in a particular region so that they do not "overpopulate" our living space. We eat them and abuse them and kill them if they inconvenience us.

I was having issues with mice getting into my car at night. Friends advised me to put poison out to kill them or put out sticky pads to trap them (which would have caused them to die slowly from starvation). I was horrified at the advice I was getting - when all it took was for me to leave the hood of my car open at night so the mice didn't find refuge inside. It's NOT all about us...and it never was. So...why do we think it is?

For those of us who feel superior - I do understand how this came about. We learned it from our culture and the habit is really not our fault. But it is our responsibility to contemplate this concept once it is mentioned to us and be accountable. Consider this: Who put us in charge of this earth? God didn't, the Buddha didn't and no other enlightened being did. So who did? We did. Our species is superior in creativity and conceptual thought. Our brain gives us that capability. We have created the most deadly weapons so we win? And all the other beings of the world have to suffer through the end results of our rage, indiscretion, arrogance and utter stupidity? We feel we should make all decisions for all beings on this planet? And they have to live with it. How is that fair?

The cows, chickens, and pigs will be eaten. The wild animals will be killed because they are a nuisance to us or they serve as a trophy. Insects will be poisoned because they bug us (pun intended) and birds are messy so let's kill them too.

Who do we think we are? God? Yes- but we are far from it.

The wrathful goddess bubbles up quickly when someone tells me they love animals and would never hurt them but picks up a burger and relishes it. Are they really that out of touch and victims of powerful propaganda that they cannot equate burger to dead animal? If I can instill one action for anyone who reads this book, it is to become a vegetarian. Please - All that talk that humans don't get enough protein without eating meat is just hogwash.

Consider our teeth. We have learned in school that predators (carnivores) have pronounced canine teeth to rip flesh and kill their prey. Do humans have pronounced canines...like cats do? No. We have very small canines and many more grinding teeth like grazing animals. We were meant to eat grains and vegetables. You may like the taste of a good burger but it's all societal conditioning. From the time we were small children, many of us were so excited to have a trip to McDonalds or Burger King for a burger, fries and coke. Realize what is happening here...all conditioning...all habits...all cultural manipulating. I say this over and over so you are aware - not to insult you. Habits are really hard to break and it's not your fault. However, after contemplating this and having even the smallest realization of what is happening....I ask for you to be accountable.

Yes...we humans are smart. But we are also capable of brutality, cheating, and manipulating the truth. We sometimes out and out lie to get what we want. We can invent new amazing things and horrible things. And we have the mind power to manifest inventions that annihilate all life and poison the land so that it is uninhabitable. We have great power of possibilities because of our rational and manipulative mind. BUT...how smart would we be if there was another true nuclear holocaust similar to what took place in Chernobyl? How many of us would survive with no electricity, no supermarket to shop for food and no fresh water. Think of that. You would only survive a day or two unless you could find a water source and good luck with that in a nuclear emergency.

It's true that animals and birds would be killed too but they know how to forage for food and take care of themselves in ways that most of us know nothing about. We are used to a life of convenience and comfort. Animals would adapt easier. But the real atrocity is that they were the innocent beings who would have to suffer for our mistakes. They suffer right now. They are innocent and the human race hurts them, eats them, disregards them and treats them like they don't have a life that is important to them.

I hope people wake up before it's too late.

Death is difficult for humans as I expect it is for those in the animal kingdom. I don't, however, profess to know something that I couldn't possibly know - like how an animal feels at the time of death. I don't even know how I will feel when my body dies. People have told me that animals are much better at death than humans and that death comes easier for them but I wonder how people arrive at that conclusion. How could they possibly know the pain and fear an animal feels during death? Is this just an attempt to rationalize that it's OK to kill an animal because they die well? Do humans de-personalize the pain and agony of animals to minimize the potential guilt we would carry as a result of the abuse and assaults against wildlife and even pets.

The beautiful, positive attributes of the human realm are kindness and altruism. And...when we are able - to be compassionate. We humans came into this realm to learn to be kind and altruistic and most religions teach us those principles. But, how many of us truly look out for those people outside our family circle?

When a tragedy hits, many of us put aside our differences and self-centered nature and help those who were crushed by an event like an earthquake, or hurricane....or 9-11. However, as soon as the upheaval subsides, we go right back to taking care of ourselves and our families until another tragedy occurs. Most people haven't learned the lesson that to be truly altruistic, we treat others and their families as if they are our own and we never see that we exert our effort to help others because they aren't "others" but part of our own. The turkeys taught me that.

HUMAN VANITY

OOHHH – Vanity ....one of my least favorite traits in a person and my favorite thing to write about. Figure that one out.

Human arrogance and vanity...where does it come from? Why do humans feel they are God on earth?

It's the ego. The ego is created when we take form and its purpose is to protect the body and our emotional well being. When we are in spirit form, we don't have the ego to contend with – there's no emotions or physical form to protect. There is so much out-of-control ego running rampant and unchecked in this world today that it is stifling...at least to me.

I met a man yesterday who told me his story. He had been a "big wig" for several companies – even managed the Arizona Cardinals and knew senators, actors, and wealthy business people. At one point, his head got too big for his britches and he was arrested for fraud and theft. He lost his business, home and family. He now rents an apartment and leases a fancy convertible. He says that his business is his asset, which means to me that he has nothing else. Even after losing everything important to him, this man still lacks humbleness. After all he had gone through, his true nature was not shining through but he sure retained an abundant supply of arrogance.

I'M A HALF-BREED

I realize my desires are so different from others of my realm. Sometimes I feel that I am in better alignment with the Animal Realm than Human...and then there are times when I'M SURE of it. Animals are real. They have no pretenses - small egos - no ulterior motives. They just want food, to procreate and live safely. Their fears are mostly of survival – unlike humans who are concerned less about their survival and more about success, money and comfort. Animals have little comfort and sometimes my heart goes out to them for having no shelter and having to forage for or kill their dinner. During the dead of summer in the desert or when the sky opens up and spews out rain or snow, I think of all the beings of the animal and bird kingdom who have little shelter and wonder how they survive. But what is admirable about them is that THEY ARE FREE - free of desire for comfort, money and prestige. They have pure, simple minds...the Minds of Enlightenment.

Some animals are very important to Humans - our pets. And our pets love us...don't they? Remember that they depend on us for their lives. If humans fail to feed them, the pets will starve. Do they really love their owners? I believe many do but how do we know for sure when our pets are not free? They depend on us for food and we depend on them for love. Is this a relationship built on freedom?

I sound like I'm really bashing the heck out of my own race ...don't I? Yes...I really am. I'm bashing them because most times I see a lack of humility and authenticity in my fellow beings. We are afraid to be real and share our deepest feelings about who we are and why we are here in this life and we focus more on getting something for ourselves and our families than living a life of integrity.

All religions teach kindness and compassion but does that mean we should practice kindness and compassion only with other humans or do the teachings propose we practice kindness with ALL LIVING BEINGS? Jesus Christ and the Buddha did not teach "Be kind and loving to other humans". They taught "be loving and kind" period. They didn't teach "Thou shall not kill other humans." The teaching was "Thou Shall not Kill" period. When Christ taught "Love others as I have loved you". "Others" to me includes humans, animals, birds, insects, reptiles, etc. - not just humans.

The most kind, compassionate, and healthy action one can take is to stop eating animals. I have no need to control others but do hold space as a role model for those of us who choose to live a compassionate life...we can at least say that we don't kill animals to relish their flesh. I hope this principle I live by is food for thought to you because it may feel uncomfortable for some folks but it is consistent and in no way...serving myself. It is for the love and respect of other beings who cohabitate with us on this earth that is currently decaying – mostly because of human disregard for the health of our home.

Try it...cut meat from your diet for one month and see how much better you feel – physically and emotionally. You will also give yourself a spiritual lift....trust me.

Crestone Mountains

LEAVING DOLORES – HELLO to CRESTONE

It was now turkey hunting season in Dolores and my heart dropped every time I heard a gunshot. The owner of the house had given permission for his friends to hunt on his property so that meant that when I was out on the porch working, I could hear gunshots at close range. Also, the hunters were traipsing around pretty near the house I was renting and just as my friends were in danger, I was also in the line of fire. I decided to fight back so every time I heard a shot I would scream out "Leave the turkeys alone, you idiot. Go away!" I even bought a bullhorn that I would set off to annoy the hunters and hopefully protect the turkeys. Finally, the police showed up at my door....of course. Punish the person who DARES to go against the current.

The policeman informed me that I was breaking the law by hindering hunters...can you believe that? I never heard anything so ridiculous but perhaps it was for safety purposes. I knew the policeman wouldn't care that I was trying to protect the turkeys so I used my safety as the reason I was annoying the hunters. I told him I worked outside on the porch and the shots were coming from all around me. I felt I was in danger. He didn't care. He told me that when I feel that I'm in danger, I should call the police. I told him – "I'm in danger. I'm notifying you now." I called the police every time the shots started and they came to the house a couple times but then stopped. In the end it was OK for the turkey hunters to kill innocent turkeys but I had no rights as an innocent bystander who didn't want to get shot. I knew that no matter how much I stood up and tried to fight city hall, it was futile. The hunting tradition was so ingrained in the people of this town that I would have had to blow it up to extinguish that awful legacy so I decided I had to leave. But – where do you go where there is not hunting allowed?

There were aspects of Dolores I loved. The trees were beautiful and the wildlife was plentiful and I would really miss the ponds and the fish but it was brutal to withstand hunting season – especially with an avid hunter as a landlord. I knew it was time to go but I didn't really know where I should live next. I had a friend who was a doctor in Crestone, Colorado so that was an option. It was a good one too because in the town of Crestone and the surrounding areas no hunting was allowed....Hallelujah!!! Crestone is a unique little town nestled at the base of the Sangre de Cristo mountains. At over 8,000 ft high, this elevation would be the highest I'd ever lived in. Would that be a problem for me? I wasn't sure at the time but I was gonna give it a heck of a try.

Packing up my belongings in Dolores wasn't a big issue since the house I had rented for a year was furnished and most of my belongings were back in Scottsdale. I was able to pack all of my belongings into my car but emotionally...I was sad and felt like I was abandoning my friends.

Leaving human friends behind in Dolores wasn't an issue but leaving my wildlife friends was extremely painful. I loved Eleanor, her mate Zeus and all the turkeys. I would miss talking with the baby eagle and all the fish I had become so fond of. I would miss the playful otters and the coyotes that visited occasionally but always were run out of town by the turkey warriors. Just as when I leave any place to move to another, the pain of leaving my wildlife friends was excruciating. But, it was time and I was up to the challenge. Onward to Crestone, Colorado - "the spiritual mecca" of Colorado....or so they say.

Bella and the Girls

CRESTONE

I arrived in Crestone in mid June and the weather was absolutely beautiful. The house I rented was quirky and small, but cute. In fact, I had to convert the garage into a living room just to have the space for my furniture – and believe me – I have moved around many times so I don't have much furniture. It was an unusual use of the garage but I'm not picky about the house I live in...I'm picky about the environment. This house was on wooded land with a creek just a short distance away so it suited me well for now. The only issue was the neighbors. People make lots of noise but I like quiet. So I constantly told myself this was temporary. I needed to live here in Crestone to decide if I wanted to make this area my home permanently.

Within the week I had traveled back to Scottsdale, loaded up my belongings into a moving truck, driven the truck back to Crestone and unloaded everything into the new dwelling – making this Crestone house my home. It had been a year since I had access to my "stuff" so it was a great homecoming to have all of me in one place.

My friend offered me an office job so I worked at her clinic four mornings a week. I had already secured another Crestone resident as a client, found a cleaning job with Colorado College, and I retained two clients still in Phoenix. I felt secure in my ability to support myself in this very tiny town.

FAIRIES

As I've already revealed, Hummingbirds are one of my favorite friends so two days after I moved into this house, there was a hummingbird feeder in the backyard and they were the first Colorado friends I made. At the peak of the summer there were in excess of 50 fairies flying around my upstairs balcony and my back yard. What a sight to behold. I'd never been around so much magic at once.

After my morning work, I would return home a little after noon and the fun for me started. I loved to sit out under the trees in the afternoons and work virtually for my Phoenix clients. It didn't take long for the hummingbirds to literally surround me - waiting for their turn at the nectar. An alpha male hummingbird claimed the back yard as his domain and soon took a liking to me. Needless to say, I was very fond of him. He would chase all the other birds away from the nectar and away from me. I even had to put up several feeders so that the other birds were able to get some nourishment because Attila (the warrior) wouldn't let them get close to "his" personal chef or the precious golden nectar.

Attila always kept me company. He was the great self proclaimed "protector of the nectar" and he was funny and sweet to me...but a warrior to the rest. Good thing I had a total of five hummingbird feeders in the yard and porch or the others would have rarely gotten any nectar and Attila would have exhausted himself protecting his turf.

Since he lived in the trees in the backyard, he was always there when I came out to work or just sit and be with the yard's wild animals. From early morning until late at night all the Fairies would flit around, fight, and drink nectar....always giving me some attention as well. I love them all but Attila is special. We have a strong bond much like what I shared with Spencer in Scottsdale. He flirts with me by fluffing up his feathers when I talk to him and lands on the low branches of trees above my head for a short chat. Such a big heart for a small bird. One afternoon I walked out in the back yard with my computer - ready to begin the second half of my work day when a humming bird was attracted to my pink shirt and started poking at my back - trying to get nectar from my shirt. In no time, Attila chased him away from me...forcefully. I knew then that he was my protector. From the moment I set foot into the back yard, Attila and I were conversing. In fact, I would talk with him in the morning before work at the clinic and then again all afternoon as I worked for virtual clients. He was so much company for me and I for him. In fact, I dreaded the time when he would leave Colorado and migrate to a warmer climate for the winter. I was told that from mid September to mid October he and the rest of the Fairies would be leaving and it was already that time frame. In fact, the nights were starting to get cold (down to the 30s) and I was concerned that he would stay too long for my sake and be in trouble for the winter. I sure didn't want him to freeze. He eventually did leave and I was both relieved (for his safety) and sad for myself. I knew I would miss him terribly.

BEN

It was dusk one fall evening and I was spending as much time as possible outside since I knew once winter hit, there would be limited available time to just sit and enjoy. I walked out the back door about 8:15 pm just to see what was happening amongst my friends. I soon noticed a "big round figure" laying at the back of my yard under a tree. I couldn't figure out what it was and I knew it wasn't there earlier. Finally, I realized that it was a bear. Why was this bear laying in my backyard? Well I guess he had to lay somewhere to rest so I just stood and watched to see what would transpire. As I've stated, I offer peanuts to the birds and I noticed that the little can I put the peanut bag in was open. Ah....I get it. This bear smelled the peanuts, opened the can, grabbed the bag of peanuts and took them under the tree for a snack.

I watched this scenario unfold for quite a while - it seemed that it was taking him a long time to eat the peanuts but I was intrigued and couldn't take my eyes off of him. Finally he stood up and slowly walked toward me. I wasn't really afraid of him until he got pretty darn close so I cleared my throat and when he saw me, he just leisurely made a right turn and mosied down to the creek. He was a good sized cinnamon colored black bear - very beautiful. Since it was near dark, I decided to investigate further the next morning. It's not a good idea to venture out into the woods at night...too many predators.

When he was gone, I smiled and thought you never have these experiences in the city and I was grateful that I was living in a place where I can relish these rare moments. Ben seemed like a good name for such a big creature...so Ben was his name.

The next day, I walked out to where Ben had been laying the evening before - obviously feasting on the peanuts in the shell. What I saw was astonishing. There laid the opened bag which was empty and a big pile of peanut shells. That amazing bear had not just eaten the peanuts whole like the deer do. This guy actually shelled them first and then ate the peanuts inside. That's pretty astonishing and I so wish I knew how he did it.

This bear experience happened right before bears hibernate in Colorado - November timeframe so I was looking forward to seeing this guy again in the spring. And I was not to be disappointed. One morning in April I had gotten up extra early and happened to look out my kitchen window to be delighted. There was "Ben" sauntering through my backyard. I was so happy to see him again. But wait...there was more. He was bigger than I remember and two cute-as-a-button cubs were following right after HER. So...I guess Ben was really Bonita! I wanted to run out there and hug Bonita's adorable kids but we all know how that would end so I restrained myself - adoring them from afar. Later that summer I caught sight of Bonita and her cubs on my trail cam - boy had they grown!!! Big and Beautiful - just like their mama!

Amos – My Heart Friend

AMOS AND HIS FAMILY

One afternoon in September, I was working on my computer (as always) when this huge mule deer - a buck - came waltzing into the yard. He had a very large set of antlers. I grew up in Pennsylvania and was raised by a man who loved wild animals (I guess I got this love of nature from my dad). He taught me from an early age to always count a buck's anter points and that would give you an indication of his age so that's the first thing I did when I encountered the magnificent animal. I counted 10 points on this big boy. He saw me right away and we both watched each other intently.

Deer are normally very shy around humans (for good reason) but here in Crestone, there is no hunting allowed. So, the animals wander from yard to yard - with no fear of getting hurt. (At least that is the reason I gave myself for this amazing animal walking right toward me.) He stopped when he was about 8 feet from my workstation under the Juniper trees and both of us gazed at one another. When he took a couple steps toward me, I began to feel a little uncomfortable – that rack was so big and I wasn't sure of what he was planning.

He stood about 6 feet from me for the longest time and just watched me with those big soft brown eyes. That was it...he captured my heart within those few minutes. I stayed seated so he didn't feel threatened and dash away. Finally, he walked away and vanished into the woods. The next afternoon he came to visit again. This time I had an apple waiting for him. I threw slices of the apple down in the grass for him to relish. The next afternoon, we repeated the same routine.

Clark, my deer friend in Pagosa Springs, loved me very much but he never felt comfortable enough to take apples from my hand; however, the next afternoon I thought I'd give it a try with this big strappin' deer. I reached out my hand and I was so amazed when he walked close to me and took the apple slice so very gently. I was excited that within three days he trusted me enough to come close and take the apple from my hand. What a love he was and his name quickly and easily came to me.....Amos. From that moment on, we both preferred the offering of food from my hand to his lips and the bond was formed between an majestic buck and myself.

Almost every afternoon Amos came for a snack. I thoroughly enjoyed his visits and he seemed to like them as well so I cut up a variety of fruits and veggies and offered them to him in a big bowl. We continued our afternoon visits for a couple months but then one day he didn't come to visit me and that day turned into months. My intuition told me that he was healthy and happy but I was perplexed at why his pattern changed. Most likely his natural instinct called him for mating season. And what an amazing specimen he was for breeding.

One especially cold day in February, I went out into the back yard to offer food to the deer as I always did and I saw a familiar face - it was Amos. After being absent for months, he had returned. I looked at him and said, "Amos...is that you?" He walked right up to me waiting for me to offer him an apple. I was so happy that my friend remembered me after many months away and felt comfortable walking right up to me again.

So my friend Amos was back and he came every day for snacks - and sometimes he came several times a day. I was a happy woman. Amos and the herd leader, Philip traveled together and the other deer paid them the highest respect. There were so many deer coming into the yard to partake of the goodies I offered, that they were eating me out of house and home. I was happy to have made some new friends: Phillip, Felix and Oscar, Bella, Half Ear, Beauty, and many more occasional visitors. I loved them all but feeding an entire herd of mule deer was taking a lot of time, energy, and money.

One of my favorite deer was a very small male yearling I named Bambino. I wasn't sure if he was a boy or girl at the time but his name seemed to fit him. He took food from my hand almost immediately...unlike the rest of the herd. Some would come very close but they didn't trust me quite enough and I didn't feel the connection with them that I had with Bambino and Amos. My spiritual guide had asked me to take good care of Bambino - he was just so little. I feared he wouldn't make it through the winter if I hadn't taken him under my wing. He had no mother to look out for him so I noticed the doe took turns nurturing him and staying close to teach him the ways of the deer. And - Amos also stepped up to be a big brother to Bambino. It was so beautiful to see.

In late February, I walked out into the yard and saw a set of antlers laying on the ground. This was a gift from Felix - one of the younger bucks. He showed up the next day with a naked head so I was pretty sure he was the gift giver. How different he looked. Next...Amos showed up one morning sans his antlers - with a small amount of blood on his cheek. He seemed to take it like a trooper - of course I'm sure he had gone through that process several times. Finally all the males lost their antlers as deer do every year and Philip was the only one with antlers still intact. And...huge antlers they were. He was a 12-point buck with a huge standing rack.

As I mentioned, Philip was the elder male of the group and all the other deer (including Amos) paid great respect to him. The relationship between Philip and Amos was quite intimate - almost like a father and son. Amos reminded me of a General reporting to his Commander - he and Philip were inseparable. One morning I was offering food and all of a sudden all the deer jumped. I looked up and one of Philip's antlers got caught in the clothesline and was on the ground. All the deer stopped and focused on Philip who appeared shaken. He wandered over to the thicket and stood away from the herd which was unusual. He stood there for about 15 minutes and was having difficulty keeping his head level. With only one antler, he was quite lopsided and looked very uncomfortable. Even when he wandered back into the yard to join the rest of the group, he was having some trouble with his equilibrium.

As Phillip rejoined his herd, Amos bowed his head down and pulled his ears back when his Commander walked by. I can't possibly know what Amos was thinking by that gesture, but it looked like a sign of respect and empathy for his Leader. It proved to me that animals have love and respect for one another. They care for one another and take their relationships very seriously.

The next day, Philip was fine but still had not dropped the other antler which had to be uncomfortable for him. I sent him healing energy constantly - asking for the other antler to painlessly fall. I had his one antler to remember him by and the set from Felix. Having a memento from the deer herd made me happy - especially since it was their leader who left it for me.

The next evening Philip showed up without the other antler. His head was naked now and he looked so relieved. So was I. I decided to search the yard in hopes that he dropped the antler in my yard, although the odds of that happening were slim since deer wander for miles on their winter route.

My son-in-law sent me a text and asked how I was doing so I returned the text and told him I was searching for Philip's other antler - although I figured I would never find it considering the odds. Justin answered me and said, "Mom...I have a feeling that Philip left it for you in the yard. He knows it would make you happy to have the full set from him." Suddenly I looked down and there was Philip's other dropped antler under a Juniper tree. I remembered he had been resting under this tree the last time I saw him in the yard. Justin was right. Philip had left his antler for me - and what an amazing rack it was. I will treasure it and display it for the rest of my life. Thank you, Philip!

It was interesting to watch the difference in deer behavior after all the males shed their antlers. The females moved closer to them, nuzzled their faces, and sniffed them. The males allowed other males to come closer. It's understandable that the males can't really come into close proximity to others when they've got so much artillery on their heads. But after dropping all that protection, I saw true caring on the parts of males, females and young deer. Amos would regularly groom Phillip and vice versa. I never beheld such intimacy between males before and I was touched that they shared it with me. Was Amos Phillip's son? I guess I'll never know but watching these two male deer caring for one another was beautiful. And...the only time they could enjoy this intimate time together was after their sets of antlers fell and before the next formed.

What have I learned from the Deer...Unconditional Love. They care for one another and everyone knows the rules. If they don't abide by the rules, there are consequences but not severe ones. They watch out for each other and for those who love them. I truly believe that Amos and the

189

others would protect me if I was in danger and for that, I am eternally grateful.

Soon - it was spring in Crestone. This was my first spring in these majestic mountains - since I arrived in June of previous year. All the creatures were exuberant - cold weather was over and fresh new green plants were peaking out of the soil. I was happy to be able to once again work outside in my yard and welcome the hummingbirds back.

A couple of times I thought I heard the distinctive hum of fairy wings so I put the 5 hummingbird feeders outside and waited. Wow...it didn't take very long. That very day, I saw my first friend and welcomed him back. Each day more and more arrived until one day I noticed a male hummingbird sitting above me - looking down. Hmmm. This bird looked like Attila and he was behaving like he was familiar with me. I called up to him, "Is that you, Attila...my sweet boy?" He fluffed his feathers and my heart jumped for joy. Here was my old friend, Attila who had returned to me this spring. I couldn't believe he found his way back to this very house but I shouldn't be surprised. If hummingbirds can migrate thousands of miles, why is it so hard to believe they could return to a favorite summer home. I was overjoyed that my friend would spend another season with me and he seemed as happy as I.

Jax

MY NEW FRIEND – JAX

One afternoon as I worked on my computer from the back yard a limping and very underweight male deer walked slowly into my yard. Since the deer were without antlers right now, I wasn't sure who this being was but he walked right up to me. He was so skinny, sick and lacked any zest for life. Once he came closer I saw that he had a huge wound on his side and one on his opposite hip. He also had a large bulbous wound on his leg. Since Amos was the only deer who would walk right up to me, I assumed this deer was really desperate for some help.

I went inside and gathered some vegetables and fruits for him and he came right up to me and took it all from my hand. He didn't hurt me in any way but his manner of taking food was different than what I was accustomed to with Amos but I thought his obvious brush with death may have changed his outlook and he was malnourished. It was pretty clear to me that this deer had been in a tussle with a predator of some kind and he was in pain. I had no idea how to help him with his pain but I knew that if I offered him food twice a day, it would give him more time to rest and he wouldn't have to forage for his food as usual. So that's what I did. I also decided to lace his food with Vitamin C. Would it help him? I didn't know but I thought it would help to fight off infection. So, twice a day he came and twice a day I offered him a big bowl of organic food. An injured, lame deer in the mountains with lots of predators around probably wouldn't bring forth a good outcome for the deer.

Day by day, he grew stronger. The wounds on his body healed and his limp was gone. The swelling on his leg remained but it didn't seem to bother him. I was so happy I could help him. My heart swelled with joy as I saw him recuperating.

One warm afternoon, I saw Amos enter my yard - looking for his snack so I cut some veggies and fruit and started out the door. What I found was not one buck but two. Both walked over to me and took apple slices from my hand. One deer was Amos but who was this second deer who was peacefully standing beside Amos? I reasoned that they must know one another or Amos would be chasing the other deer out of the yard. Both deer took turns as I offered them food from my hand.

So, who was this deer I had helped to heal? Why he felt comfortable coming to me and taking food from my hand is a mystery but I guess he needed help and his instinct told him I would help him. As mentioned before, he took food differently from Amos - less gentle and a bit impatient so I decided to name him Jax after a character (Jax Teller) on the TV series, Sons of Anarchy. If you've ever watched the series, you'll know why I named him Jax....he's beautiful but just a little bit dangerous.

A friend of mine watched as I cared for the deer. "You are so selfless, Tara", she said to me one day. You buy organic vegetables and fruit for this deer and make sure you add vitamin C and always make sure you are home to offer food to him.....So selfless."

I thought about what she said and replied, "I feel that I was being kind - not selfless. It is so very easy to be kind to those in the animal kingdom. They don't ask for much. This guy came to me because he knew I would help and I'm happy to do so."

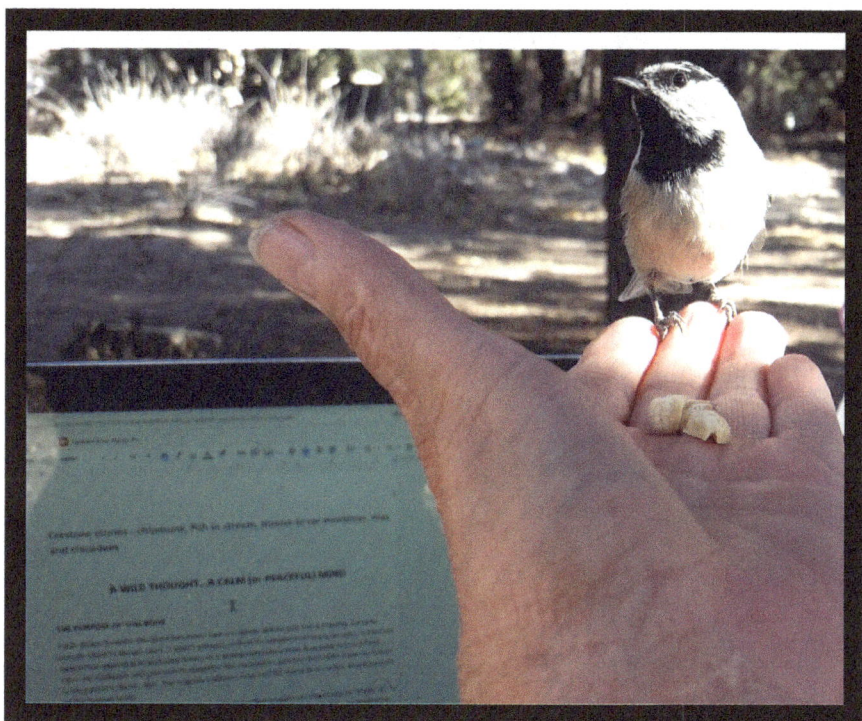

Chickadees

THE LITTLE GUYS

Living at the base of a mountain that stretches above 14,000 brings an assortment of small animals and birds. They are all precious to me and very individual.

Some of my beautiful friends are the Stellar Jays, Rocky Mountain Blue Jays, Robin Red Breasts, Magpies, and so many other birds I have not yet identified. My favorite birds are the Chickadees and White Breasted NutHatches (Max and Big Max) because they swoop down and take peanuts from my hand. They first land on my hat, which is an alert to me that they expect a peanut. I stretch out my hand and they fly onto my wrist and help themselves to the peanuts in the palm of my hand. When I work outside (on warm October days) I don't get a lot of work done with them around but I enjoy it immensely. All my animal and bird friends surround me when I have the magic food....PEANUTS.

Mortimer - the Squirrel

By the time my daughter Angelique was a toddler, she already had a great love for wildlife and she made friends with as many as would allow her near. One of her primary friends was Mortimer the Gray Squirrel. She and I both had a close connection to Mortimer.

I made it a practice to meditate every morning and I did so out on the front porch. I would place unshelled peanuts around me so that Mortimer would smell the peanuts and feel comfortable to come close to grab them. All three of us became friends and Mortimer grew very comfortable in our company.

One morning Angelique came into the kitchen and asked, "Mommy can I have a peanut for Mortimer?" I said, "Of course - here you go." She took the peanut and threw it into the dining room. "Why did she do that?", I wondered. Finally it hit me that Mortimer might possibly be in the dining room. I ran in and saw that devilish little squirrel shelling and eating the peanut that Angelique tossed to him. Of course, I felt the need to escort Mortimer out of the dining room and explained to Angelique that we feed our wild friends outside...not inside. It was funny and I'll never forget Mortimer.

So...here in Crestone another precious little squirrel made friends with me and in honor of Angelique's relationship with her squirrel friend when she was 3 years old, I named this little guy "Mortimer" and he is just as cute as the one who played with my beautiful little girl many years ago.

One evening in October we had a freak snowfall which dropped about a foot of snow. In the middle of the night I awoke to a flapping sound...had no idea of what it was. When I turned on the light, this being flew down the steps to the first story. I searched and searched but couldn't find this elusive being so I decided to watch a little TV and try to get back to sleep.

About 20 minutes into my movie, I heard some rustling in some boxes near me so I investigated. Low and behold, there was a bat in the box near my chair. I quickly closed the lid and trapped the bat inside. Whew...that was close. Wouldn't want to be running around the house in the middle of the night trying to catch a bat.

I've never been in close proximity to a bat and had no idea of how to care for it so the next day I called an expert who told me to just keep him in the box (with air holes, of course) and wait for a warmer day to release him. She explained that he would probably hibernate and that bats could remain in that state for quite some time. I was concerned that he would be in the box with no food and water so I slid in a couple peach slices and some apples.

Within 4 days, the temperature had returned to normal so I took the bat outside and opened the box. He was so cute - hanging upside down and hibernating as the expert had predicted. Within minutes of the fresh air hitting him, the bat was in flight. Another amazing experience.

THE MOUSE WHO LOVED COFFEE

If you will remember, the whole time I lived in Dolores I escorted mice out of the house - on a daily basis. I swear they came back - even though I took them at least a mile away. I love all animals but I have to admit, I got a bit tired of mice capture and was relieved when I moved from Dolores.

In Crestone I never had mice in the house or in my car - no matter how cold the winter night was, so it was a surprise when I found mouse droppings in my car one morning. Hmmmm. I don't really mind sharing the car with some furry friends but in the past I had experience with rats chewing the wires in my car and I really didn't want to revisit that nightmare. I tried all the deterrents that are advertised and still the furry guys visited my car (which was warmer than the outside weather early in the spring). I thought it was odd that they didn't enter my car in the winter but in the spring when the weather was warmer. I guess I was not a mouse whisperer.

I captured a few mice inside my car and relocated them but one morning I was in for a big surprise. The morning was just like other mornings. I sat my purse on the passenger seat as I entered my car and placed my coffee latte in the cup holder.
The day before I had stopped at the convenience store and bought some spicy almonds - I love 'em! I accidentally dropped three of them on the

floor of the car as I was eating. I didn't want to eat them after being on the floor and also didn't want to throw them on the ground for the animals to eat since they were so spicy. So, I placed them in the cup holder and thought I would remove them when I exited the car but I forgot. When I put my coffee latte in the cup holder, I noticed the spicy nuts were gone and thought, "Ut Oh...the guy who ate them must need some water."

On my way to work a mouse jumped onto the passenger seat and I caught the movement out of the corner of my eye. I wasn't really surprised that there was a mouse in the car but this guy was a fairly large, unusually beautiful field mouse. I was shocked, however, when he hopped into my purse. I thought I could pull the car over and capture him in my purse. That way I could escort him out of my car.

But this little guy wasn't having any of it. When I made a gesture to close the purse, he jumped out and ran back to the rear of the car...where? I had no idea.

I decided to go home and get one of my live traps so that while I was at work, I could probably capture him and then set him free in the field across from work. I turned the car around and headed back home. In a couple minutes, he jumped back on the passenger seat and was running around the seat and the floor below it. I pulled over again but he evaded me this time as well.

Finally, I returned home and pulled into the driveway, opened all the doors (in case he wanted to do me a favor and exit on his own) and then was preparing to go into the house and grab the live trap.

All of a sudden, I looked into the car and this little devil was on top of my sippy cup filled with the morning coffee latte and he was drinking my latte. This guy really had some nerve and caused me to laugh out loud. His love of sweet coffee gave me the leverage to remove him from the car by grabbing the coffee cup and walking him over to the water dish and shooing him off. I guess it was much to his liking or his poor little mouth was still on fire from eating those spiced nuts....live and learn.

In the spring, summer and fall, I spend a lot of time in my backyard among the trees communicating and playing with my little friends – as well as my huge friends like Amos and Jax. Even in the winter, I try to spend at least an hour with them in the warmest part of the afternoon unless it is utterly frigid. I would encourage all of you readers to consider spending more time in nature and with the animals and birds. You may be surprised at how much better you feel on a day to day basis.

I cannot express how much I appreciate them and the amount I have learned from them. They are truly spiritual beings with very free minds and that is a breath of fresh air for me.

WOLVES – MASTERS OF COOPERATION

The word "Wolf" brings about a multitude of reactions from human beings. Many people are awe-struck by them and others are scared to death. No matter what your feeling, they invoke the most basic, primordial instincts in many of us and their culture is built firmly on Altruism and Cooperation.

While I was still living in Scottsdale, I joined a wildlife protection group who were fighting for the rights of wolves which are extremely misunderstood in this country. Their population has dwindled to next to nothing in the continental United States and they constantly need to fight for their right to exist. Their decline is not a result of other predators, or disease, or starvation but from the hatred of human beings. Not many people really "get" wolves. Instead there is alot of fear and hatred that is not based on fact and is totally unwarranted.

One huge reason I wanted to leave Scottsdale and live in the mountains was to be near wolves so I started looking for a home in the western states like Montana and Wyoming - wilderness areas where wolves roamed. Basically, I just wanted to be near them and make friends with a pack.

Instead of finding a beautiful area that kindly supported wolf populations, I found ranchers who had no tolerance for even talking about wolves. One morning, I decided to meet some of these men to get a feel for their philosophy on wolves so I visited the local diner for breakfast. As I had hoped, there was a large table of middle to older-aged men having breakfast and chewin' the fat.

For a week, I frequented this diner and witnessed the breakfast ritual of these ranchers and greeted them with a friendly "Hello" every morning. On the 7th morning, I decided to talk with them for a few minutes. I walked up and said, "Hello, gentleman. How are you all today?" "Do you see any gentleman here?", one jovial man said. They all laughed and I chuckled right along with them.

We made small talk for a bit and then I asked the question, "I heard there was a man here in town that had a pet wolf and I'm thinking of doing the same. Do you know him or where I can find him?

One rancher quickly spoke up - aggressively, "There's no man in this area who would dare bring a darn wolf into town. The only good wolf is a dead wolf!" Wow...I was stunned at his nasty tone. But the other men in the breakfast club quickly agreed with him.

I later spoke with the owner of the diner about my experience with these men and he told me that the community's hatred of wolves "was in their DNA". This attitude had been passed down from father to son and on and on. It all stemmed from the "olden days" when wolves killing their livestock would have devastated a ranch but now the government subsidized ranchers who lost cattle to predators. So that wasn't the root of the hatred anymore. The habit of hating wolves that was passed down for generations was the culprit.

"You're kidding? These guys are still mad at wolves even though they will be paid for any cattle that are lost?", I asked a bit indignantly. "Yep", Raymond answered, "old habits die snail slow."

At that moment, I knew this area was not the place for me so I left that very day and traveled around different areas in Montana, and Wyoming – getting the same attitude of hatred for such a beautiful and altruistic animal. So I went into Washington state and found a lesser degree of indignation since there were many Native American reservations there. But the lack of state protection of wolves in the northwest in general was dismal and pushed me out of the area.

When I arrived in Pagosa Springs, Colorado, I asked my neighbors where I would find wolves and was told by several authorities that "There are no wolves in Colorado." Hmmm. I wonder if the wolves knew that. And...I was aware that within the last couple of years these wise beings had been reintroduced into northern Colorado – into Rocky Mountain State Park. What I knew about wolves was that these fine animals can literally change the ecology of an environment. If you want to see a miracle, watch a short video called "How Wolves Change Rivers". This documentary speaks about the miraculous healing that took place in Yellowstone National Park in 1995 when wolves (who had previously been annihilated) were reintroduced into the park. The reason the wolves were reintroduced was that since there were no major predators in the park, the elk and deer population had literally destroyed the vegetation. Humans were not able to control the overpopulation and so the decision was made to re-introduce the wolves. The video further explains that when the ecological balance is disturbed, an entire area can be in danger or even devastated. In this case, the ecological balance was restored thanks to the wolves.

My gut told me there were wolves around my house and when I walked out onto my deck one morning - only a week or so after moving to Pagosa Springs - I was sure that the guttural, howl I heard was that of a wolf. The cry of a coyote is just not the same. Once you hear a wolf howl, you'll never be the same again. It awakened a primordial, ancient part of me. When I saw a wolf print in the snow in my backyard a month later, I knew for sure that wolves wandered the San Juan Mountains. I could feel them.

Wolves adhere to a "wolf hierarchy", have a lot of integrity, and are extremely altruistic within their pack. We can all learn valuable lessons in leadership and cooperation from wolves.

For example:

When traveling or hunting, the old and sick wolves walk in front to set the pace.

The next group are among the strongest wolves of the pack. They protect the front side from attack.

The middle group is fully protected. They comprise the majority of the wolf pack.

The group behind them is among the strongest and they protect the back side.

The last wolf in the group is the leader. He keeps the pack tight and on the same path. He is ready to run in any direction to protect his pack and also ensures that no one is left behind.

In a wolf pack, being a leader is not about being in the front. It's about taking care of one's members - one's community. It's one of the truest forms of altruism I've encountered. A wolf community is logically and altruistically structured as well as any human military operation. The leader protects the flank and makes sure no members are hurt or left behind. The leader's main goal is to protect his pack - not to win a battle. He also monitors how and when members partake of a kill when there is food available. He makes sure that no matter what the rank, each wolf member gets his/her share of the food.

Within a couple of days of moving into the house on the side of the mountain in Pagosa Springs, a neighbor told me of an incident involving a young male cougar. It seems that this young stud went on a joyride killing spree and killed my next-door neighbor's lama, two goats, and an alpaca. He didn't eat any of them - just killed them for fun. That act is really unusual in the animal realm. So, since it was a concern that he would also start going after humans, the young cougar was hunted and killed.

While animals rarely behave in this way, we humans have an escalating incidence of this in our society. Just read the papers or listen to the news. Someone is killing, maiming, robbing or drugging every single day.

Like most predators, wolves only kill what they need to eat and they work together to accomplish their goal so that none of the pack are injured. Then they feed their families and themselves. They are altruistic, nurturing and willing to fight to the death to defend the pack against a threat.

I'm very aware of why I love wolves so much. It's also interesting to discover why so many other people who join the wildlife protection groups are intrigued by them as well. What wolf trait is so appealing and feared at the same time by humans?

The answer is FREEDOM". We humans are extremely repressed with so many societal and religious rules, laws and moral codes that we are forced to live by. We are so tied up by obligations and responsibilities for both career and family that we have little time to investigate our inner free heart and mind. When we come in contact with a being who has a mind that is totally FREE, we long for that same opportunity. That deep guttural, primal, innate animal in all of us is awakened a bit. Wolves, if nothing else, are free spirits and perhaps we see that nature in them and want it for ourselves.

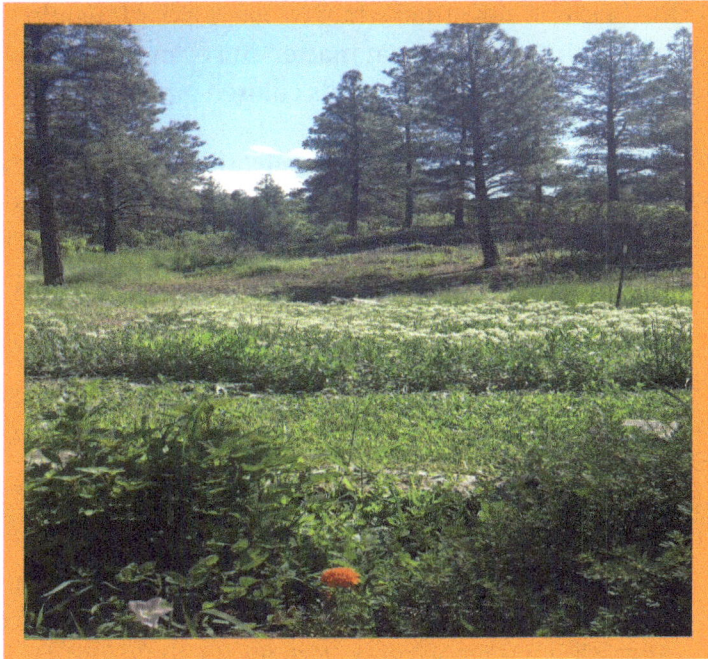

FREE THE MIND

COLOR MY LIFE

As I've stated many times throughout this book, animals operate more on intuition than cognition like we humans do. A larger cognitive brain gives human beings a way to create and bring those ideas into fruition. This aspect of our existence is what created our societies in all their glory. We don't have to live exposed in the forest like animals do – we have homes that are very comfortable and inventions that make our lives much easier. BUT our cognitive powers change our perspective from simple to complex.

In just 50 years our world has changed enormously. As a teenager, I didn't have a cell phone, an electric car, a big screen TV, etc. Life was simpler. Is life "better" now than when we were kids? It would take a whole separate book to explore that matter and even then, it would all come down to one's perspective.....one's colored glasses.

There are as many views on birth, life and death as there are leaves on the Juniper Tree I'm sitting under. So, which view is "right" and which is "wrong"? The way it appears, every individual believes his/her view is "right" and other views are "wrong". However, if you are a logical person, you will conclude that this perspective cannot possibly be true. Beliefs are very subjective. And they are not real because they change like the wind. Therefore, we will say that all spiritual, religious or cultural beliefs are "right for us" and not "right".

I've debated religious ideals with many people and one thing is consistent: Even though a person will proclaim to be "tolerant" of other religions, most still believe they are "right" and those poor souls who don't believe similarly will go to hell. Even the word "tolerant" emits a negative connotation, in my opinion. Perhaps we could just say "To each his own". We humans have a strong need to express our opinions even though others really couldn't care less about them. So...why do we waste our energy?

No matter what our religious or cultural beliefs, these concepts have shaped our views and our lives. Christians believe that when a baby is born, the child is innocent. Buddhists believe that the child comes into this life with a karmic bank that will affect how he/she sees the world. Atheists believe that a child is born, lives life, and dies and there is no afterlife or reincarnation. To me....no matter what your religious or cultural ideas or what your view is on living your life – if we have a clean slate when we are born, that slate gets mighty dirty within a very short time. And if we have lived multiple lives, our slate is really messy.

For discussion purposes, let's assume a newborn child is innocent. How long do they retain that purity? Most people see newborns as cute and precious but by the time they are 2 years old (the terrible twos) they are capable of controlling parents, manipulating their environment and down-right ornery behavior. I've heard parents say "I can't wait until they grow out of this stage!" Do children grow out of the "terrible twos" stage or do they learn to be more subtle in their controlling behaviors?

Every single experience we have in this life (and in previous lives if you believe in reincarnation) "colors" how we see the world. Past experience impacts our views and habits and molds how we interact with others. Those entities that color our world are our culture (society), our religion, our education and those people we interact with. Our parents have been shaped similarly so they will perpetuate the ideals they learned and pass those habits and beliefs on to us. These powerful influences shape who we are....period.

We human beings tend to be concerned mostly with our own happiness and the happiness of those close to us - our family and friends. Other than that, we tend to turn a blind eye on those we don't know.

Animal species tend to look after one another without expecting anything in return. I watched as my friend Phoebe, who was a beautiful ground squirrel, cared for a stranger. Phoebe and her two children made my back yard their home and they were "Johnny on the spot" when the peanut can rattled. I would hide some peanuts under the wood steps to the house so that the jays and other larger birds wouldn't find them - and Phoebe soon found them for her dining pleasure.

One day a newcomer to the yard started stealing peanuts of his own. The bigger birds were happy to share with Phoebe and her kids but adding a new mouth to the mix was too much for them and they became intolerant of this intruder. I'm pretty sure Phoebe wasn't familiar with him because she kept her distance but when the birds started picking on him, she stepped in and defended him. I believe her altruistic behavior was innate.

Anarchy is a scary word for many people but the term really speaks of freedom. Emma Goldman says it well, "Anarchism stands for the liberation of the human mind from the dominion of religion, liberation of the human body from the dominion of property, and liberation from the shackles and restraint of government."

I have no desire to write anything negative about cultural and religious practices because everyone has a right to believe what they will but if a group of humans uses these practices to control another group of people, then I disagree with that. If we truly take a close look, we will see that very thing has happened all through our history and is still taking place.

The animal kingdom operates under much less stringent and overbearing rules and constraints than humans do. Therefore, they have much freer minds. I'm not proposing that we give up our homes and live in the forest. I'm also not recommending that we just start breaking the rules of our culture. In that light, we would end up incarcerated or dead.

What I'm recommending is that we take steps to see the Truth. There's really only one thing that is real and permanent and that is the Enlightened part of us - our True Nature. We can take steps to reveal our True Nature and Free Our Minds of so many rules that camouflage who we truly are....spiritual beings who are experiencing lives within physical bodies. If we can always remember that and not get so caught up in the "right" and "wrong" of everything we encounter in our lives, then our minds will be freer. It is our birthright to see the Truth.

If we can let go of wanting to be "right" and "winning rather than losing", then we will be happier. If we can begin to see all other living beings as precious, then we will also see the preciousness in ourselves. Altruism is a key to a peaceful mind if we can find it in our hearts to care for others - whether they be human, animal, insect, plant, etc. ALL living beings are precious and EQUAL. We humans have had a huge hand in the destruction of our planet. It is happening right now and the unfairness about that is that the animal kingdom hasn't taken part in that destruction. They live in harmony with other flora and fauna in this world and still they have to deal with the fallout of our ignorant mistakes. We are the great destructors and still we make our animal brothers and sisters our beasts of burden, our food source, and the targets of our constant frustration. The very least we can do for them after all the pillaging we've done to their homes is to be kind to them.

We have created complex societies for ourselves that keep getting more and more complicated. How can we be free of all these entanglements? Since animals are our insight into the simple plan, watching them shows us what is necessary in life and what is a result of the control our society exerts over us. Animals have little desire...they need food and they procreate. Their lives are just as important to them as our lives are to us. They create simple communities and companionship but other than that, they have few rules.

Animals have simple, free minds and by being part of their lives, we can learn to free our minds as well. Observing them and the way they live is the basis of my method to resolve one's karma - "Free the Mind". I owe them a great appreciation and will forever be grateful for the teachings they shared with me.

AWARENESS IS THE ANSWER

Anyone who studies Buddhism, meditation or any of the healing arts uses the word "awareness" over and over again. When I was a Baby Buddhist (my first year of study) I heard the word "awareness" so many times but when I asked people to explain it, they fell short. That meant to me that they didn't truly understand its meaning.

It is difficult to express the true meaning of awareness because it is beyond words. The Buddha (after becoming enlightened) said he could not teach others how to become Enlightened. He couldn't put the process into words. People had to experience it for themselves. Awareness has to be practiced and finally experienced as well because it is the first step toward Enlightenment. But finding one's way to that experience is sometimes like groping around in the dark to find the pen you dropped.

Why do so many of us have difficulty living in the present moment? One reason may be that we don't totally know, love and accept ourselves. We rush through our lives and never ask "Where am I rushing to?" No matter where we go, there we are! Once we get down to the core of this issue and learn to know and accept ourselves, many of our pressing problems will be resolved and our lives will be transformed. And since we are kinder to ourselves, we will also be kinder to others and people will respond more positively to us.

By observing animals, I soon experienced the sense of awareness they possess. Without keen awareness, their lives would be very short. There's always a predator waiting for an unassuming being to let his/her guard down. And a predator without awareness, will not have a meal to keep him/her alive. Animals are masterfully aware so it's only fitting that I learned from the Masters about "Living in the Now."

Some Practical Tips for Living in the "NOW" as I learned from the Animal Masters

Here are some practical tips for living in the present moment - "animal style". They will be very helpful for us in our daily lives.

Be mindful of your breath. There is no need to use sophisticated breathing techniques - just pay attention to your breath. Breathe deeply and slowly - from the belly and enjoy the process. This is such an easy thing to do. Try it and see that your life will be more peaceful and calm. If you have a family pet, observe them as they sleep - they will exhibit deep "belly breathing."

Meditate on a regular basis. This exercise won't bring you to the door of Enlightenment, but it can lower blood pressure, ease the stress of the day, bring the mind peace, calmness and clarity, and give one a general sense of wellbeing. If there's one thing you can do to benefit your life it would be to calm and lighten your mind. Animals don't formally practice meditation but if you watch them while resting peacefully, they calm their minds in their own special ways. Observe a deer chewing his/her cud while lying under a tree in the afternoon....that is a serene practice.

Be mindful of your physical feelings. Ask yourself: "How do I feel right now? Am I sitting in a comfortable position? Are my shoes and clothes comfortable? What is my body trying to tell me?" So many of us go through our lives ignoring our feelings. But one day the body will refuse to be ignored another minute and we will get sick. At that point we will be forced to get in touch with our feelings and finally be open to guidance and valuable suggestions.

Animals and birds are constantly in tune with their physical bodies. At a moment's notice, they may have to flee so they are always in tune with their environment and the beings surrounding them and they can switch into motion at the flash of an eye.

Slow your life down a bit. Most times, there is no need to rush. Sometimes we are so afraid of being late for an appointment, job, etc. that we don't realize the world does not depend upon us for its survival. Of course, it is good to be on time but a wise person utilizes careful planning instead of rushing. As you plan your day, give yourself more time to do the important things and eliminate the non-important things as much as possible. If you have time to do the less important things in your life, do them. Otherwise, don't rush. And if you ARE late for an appointment, don't burden yourself further by feeling guilty.

Be grateful for the delays. When you are in a traffic jam or standing in a line, try not to be angry or upset. Realize that this delay is a gift. You have a chance to be alone with yourself for a few minutes, without distraction. Watch your breath and physical feelings and try to relax. Think about how precious your life is and appreciate it fully. Smile to yourself. Look at people around you and know they also have this precious human life. In an instant, your tension will subside and you will get in touch with the joyous spirit of the present moment.

Animals don't get upset when they are delayed. They do have their routines but they're able to flow through their day like water in a stream. While feasting on delicacies in my yard, the deer will sprint from the area when the neighbor's dog starts to bark but they return when the coast is clear and continue munching away. I don't really think they are upset by the delay. They are just taking care of their physical safety first and then returning when the coast is clear.

Lotus Flower – Symbol of Enlightenment

WHY I FELT COMPELLED TO WRITE THIS BOOK?

As I stated in the first sentence of this book, when I see a tragedy, I have to take action. The abandonment of the human spirit is a tragedy. Like the Anarchists... I need to be free. How about you? I've learned that one will NEVER be free until one's mind is free. Only when the mind is free, can we be at peace.

I've made friends with many wild animals and there is one thing about them that is consistent across all the species I've had the honor to know: Their instincts and intuition are stronger than any other part of them. That's what keeps them alive. Instinctively, they know what they need to do no matter what their feelings are about me or anyone else and they live by those instincts rather than emotions.

Attila loved me as deeply as I loved him. But when it came time for him to migrate to warmer territory....he left. He did procrastinate a bit and was the last hummingbird to leave my trees. I was getting concerned that he would freeze. But..in the final analysis, he knew what was best for him and he was gone.

Have you ever wondered where the birds and animals go for shelter when there are torrential downpours and when the sky dumps 20 inches of snow? Rarely do they seek shelter in or under a man-made structure. I've always had houses with large porches and I never saw any animal or bird seek shelter there in bad weather. They find shelter in the woods. They need to be free. And they know how to take care of themselves.

No matter how close I got with a wild animal, they never became "tame". Never. No matter how much nectar I offered the hummingbirds or how much popcorn I offered the turkeys or how many fruits and vegetables I offered the deer, in the end, they did not feel beholden to me. They appreciated the gesture but they didn't compromise who they were in order to receive it. That trait touched my heart and I learned so much from them. In fact, I never met anyone in the animal kingdom who didn't teach me an important lesson.

This wild nature in animals and birds can never be erased. The same principle is true for human beings and that's why we sometimes break down from the pressure of everyday life. That's why many women are intrigued by "bad boys" and dangerous liasons. We humans still have that wild nature. So, why did we allow our freedom to be snatched away from us? We compromise our integrity many times a day. We hold our tongues to keep our jobs so that we can buy new houses and cars. We allow our spouses to speak to us with contempt and disrespect just so we don't have to go through the expense of divorce. We allow our children too many concessions in their lives when they are not mature enough to competently make important decisions.

Being extremely restrained by our society may be worth the daunting effect on our spirit if (in the end) we would be free. But we're not. We are far from it. Our government tells us what to do. Our religion tells us what to do. Our friends and family do everything in their power to keep us in line. So where are WE after all of this? Who are we? Sadly, we have no idea.

In this world today there are unprecedented levels of crime, drug use, and mental illness. Many people have more money than they know what to do with and they squander it buying things they don't need. Others are poor and struggle day and night just to feed their families. So a majority of our country spends their time on matters of the material world...not on uncovering who they really are. Who are we? We are spiritual beings in a physical body having a physical experience. REMEMBER: We are spiritual beings FIRST.

The tragedy is that we never get anywhere because our physical life takes up too much time. Many of us travel and we have been to Italy, Cabo, Hawaii...but have we ever been to US? Wars are fought and battles are won but have we ever won ourselves? Do we know who we really are?

I want to be and WILL be free like the wolves....what do you want?

Let's face it...we all know that life is suffering. We are born crying, we get sick, we grow old and we die and in between all of this, we try to find some happiness. But happiness is fleeting and gives way to the routine of living. I'm not being fatalistic - only realistic.

If any of us are serious about easing our own suffering and the suffering of others, we can tap into the secret weapon - Altruism. There are many people who walk this path and many organizations who do the same. When there is a tragedy, we humans are right there to offer our help. That's the truly great part of humankind - our willingness to help others. When there is a flood, a tsunami, an earthquake or a terrorist attack, humans rise to the occasion - partly because of our genuine kindness for others but there is also a little bit of ego in our action....which makes us feel good about ourselves. "I'm a good person...I helped those people in the flood."

Ask yourself, "Am I taking this altruistic action to feed my ego or am I purely wanting to help others?" When we extend altruism and loving kindness to a being who will not praise us for helping them and we have nothing to gain from helping them, our egos are put to the test.

When we extend our kindness to help those wild animals we don't even know and who cannot benefit us in any way, we are truly serving an altruistic attitude. They will take your kindness and probably not give you anything in return. That, my friend, is a beautiful display of true altruism. And when you practice it, you'll soon see who you truly are.

Too many of we humans take nature very much for granted. We see a fly on the counter and grab the swatter. We see a spider in the corner and kill it. We see bird dirt or evidence of mice and immediately take actions to eliminate those "nuisances". Why? Because they inconvenience us. I am ashamed to be a human when it includes heinous acts such as trophy hunting, needless abuse of animals by humans, or killing innocent beings because they piss us off.

Not only do we kill those in the animal kingdom, we cut down millions of acres of rainforest – the very beings that keep us alive - in order to raise steers for us to kill and eat. Who left us in charge? We are foolish rulers because the actions we have taken for our own convenience and pleasure are the very actions that will kill us one day. For example: We cut down the rainforests. Now there's no oxygen in the world....so we die.

Nature never lies and it will not deceive. It is naked. It is what it is. It can be harsh at times – especially when it serves as a lesson for us. Although we try our best to be in charge, NATURE CANNOT be CONTROLLED. We can't even control our own lives so how can we think we will control nature? Unless we have a Free mind, we are like a bag flapping in our own karmic wind. The only way to stop that karmic disturbance is to calm the mind and then we will realize **we are NOT our thoughts, our desires or our fears. We ARE far more than that.**

As sentient beings, we do still have the Pure Mind but our ego mind is far more active and vocal. The ego mind provides us with a lot of busy work and busy thoughts. What will I make for dinner tonight? What if my husband leaves me? Will my kids grow up to be responsible adults or will they succumb to drug use or alcohol? Will I get fired or laid off as a result of a corporate consolidation? All are distractions from our true mission on earth.

We believe we possess free will but do we really? Can we control our lives and others around us? We can work very hard for a corporation and then get thrown to the side by a corporate layoff. I know it very well because it happened to me. You can love your spouse every minute of the day and do everything possible to make them happy but that doesn't mean they will stay with you or that the two of you will be happy. YOU CANNOT CONTROL other people and truthfully, there's not a lot of control you have over yourself because your karmic bank will pull you according to your perception and habits. What truly controls us the most is our karmic bank from the past and this bank has been accumulating with interest since the beginning of time...with positive and negative charged aspects.

Once we have this body, we create all sorts of habits of the body, mind and speech. We protect our pride like it was the most valued lover. But..what is our pride? Have you ever seen it? It's true we have all experienced it but it's not easily described. It's all about the ego mind and how it wants to protect, nurture and satisfy our physical bodies. In all of this self-satisfaction, we become confused, unhappy and unsure as to how to move forward spiritually. When will we have enough money....enough food...enough love? If we leave it up to the ego, there will never be a time when we are truly satisfied.

Nature: The trees, streams, animals, birds, etc. are the answer to reevaluating who we are and why we are here. My time on the mountain drove that fact home to me. I was in the middle of raw nature...so beautiful it made me cry and still I was unhappy. I asked myself every day, "How can it possibly be that I have everything I've ever wanted and still I am unhappy?" I realized that no matter how much goodness I had in my life, I chose to desire something I didn't have - whether it be a mate, someone to adore me..whatever. In Pagosa Springs, I was living in one of the most beautiful and magical places I ever lived. And still I cried almost every day...until I shed that skin. I realized that nature is the answer because it has no desires. It just IS. And in order for me to be at peace, I had to shed my desire for things I didn't need. Many times we want what we don't have. Sheryl Crow sang it beautifully in her song *Soak Up The Sun*- "It's not having what you want...it's wanting what you've got."

So, seeing the simplicity of nature helps us learn that most of the things we want so much are things we just don't need. We may feel happy when we first buy a new house, car, etc. but after a short time, the luster of a new possession goes away. The only thing that gives us a true sense of peace and contentment is the absence of drama...the absence of a busy life....the absence of desire. We are light beings and experiencing who we truly are brings us to a state of contentment. Watch the animals.....

Communing and interacting with nature - mountains, streams, beaches, trees, wild animals and birds, snakes, turtles and insects will show you who you are. Animals and birds don't say thank you when you give them a morsel of food. In fact, they beg - and quite frankly, demand more. They may appreciate your gesture but we cannot understand their language. Therefore, interacting with wild animals is the true test of non-egotistical true-to-the-heart altruism. It is very easy to practice once we realize that we are not superior to other beings, only different. If you are able to practice kindness and altruism with nature, YOU WILL cultivate the behavior of a Bodhisattva (an Enlightened Being who returns to the physical world to help all living beings.)

We humans seek love and approval from our families, friends, peers and superiors. The Beatles sang... "All you need is love". But love is not all you need if you seek Enlightenment. If you seek Enlightenment, FREEING THE MIND IS THE ANSWER....it's all you need.

This practice is very simple...but it's not easy....

The first step to lightening your Mind is to peacefully and respectfully let go of preconceived notions, the burden of obligations, and moral repression. and governmental restraints. Being with nature is being free of mind and body. Watch the animals...they will show you the way. All you need to do is bring with you some morsels of food and a lot of patience because wildlife has learned not to trust humans - it's etched into their DNA. But with patience, you will find the most adorable friends with the purest of minds and you will learn from them. And you will thank them with all your heart when you feel peaceful and content again.

BRINGING IT ALL TOGETHER

Thank you all for reading this book. It has been my honor to share it with you.

I am aware that throughout this book the human race took a bit of a beating in my beliefs and writing. However, I haven't lost faith in we humans....I'm just disappointed in our evolution.

When I was a first-year Dharma student, I read lots of Buddhist books and Sutras. In many of the writings it was expressed that of the 10 realms of existence, the human realm is the most expedient place to become Enlightened. The reasons behind that philosophy are because humans don't have to spend most of their existence trying to survive and because our brains are more conceptual than other realms. However, the complex, conceptual ego mind creates a big mess for most of us. Many humans have evolved into beings who are more interested in the physical world than that of the spiritual. We tend to believe what we see with our eyes instead of what our intuition and wisdom tells us.

As we rely more on our conceptual mind rather than our pure (True) Mind, we drift further and farther away from our True Nature - our Enlightened State. This phenomenon is actually pushing us away from the very reason we came into this life. As I've stated throughout the book, we humans have a much more complicated mind than that of animals. That's positive for inventions and the cyber age but it moves us away from our spiritual nature. **The more simple the mind....the more Enlightened the individual.**

On a negative note: The human mind is very complicated. On a positive note: We can change the mind and change our outlook. Since our ego minds can change, all we have to do is take the steps to enjoy a freer mind....less complicated and more simple. Actually, we don't have to create anything new. We need to undo....unwind....and simplify. We "take away from" rather than "add to".

Rather than harming nature and wild animals or considering that we rule over them, we can observe and respect them - in all their glory. After all....we are truly part of Nature as a whole so we are their brothers and sisters. By observing them, we will learn a simpler way of existence. We are capable of realizing how karma is created and we can resolve that entanglement. In other words, we can realize how we got into this mess and we can get ourselves out of it. **We can do it. I have faith in us**....it only **takes just a small turn of the head!**

REMEMBER: You are first and foremost a spiritual being who came into this life for a physical experience. Own your Place....Spiritually.

SPIRITUAL ACKNOWLEDGEMENT

I would not have written this book without the excitement and encouragement of my Mother of the Heart – Mrs. Miriam Kelly. BUT...I COULD NOT have written this book without the teachings and support of my Spiritual Mother – who will remain anonymous. She has asked me not to mention her name and I respectfully follow her wishes. I have promised to serve her life after life in any way I can and that vow is what brought me to this life, enabled me to give birth to my daughter (who will also serve our Spiritual Mother), and continue my work teaching FREE the MIND.

MAY ALL BEINGS REALIZE ENLIGHTENMENT

ABOUT THE AUTHOR

Tara Hoffman has encountered and studied many spiritual approaches to enlightenment, has been a student of spiritual leaders such as His Holiness the Dalai Lama and His Holiness Sakya Trizin, and has studied Buddhism for over 20 years. She has vast experience in teaching FREE the MIND to all beings who request it.

When Tara began to see the absolute purity and simplicity in Nature and wild animals such as deer, hummingbirds, hawks, wolves, honey bees and wild turkeys, she realized that the animal mind is very simple – less complicated than that of humans. She remembered a question a student asked of His Holiness the Dalai Lama: "Honorable one....are you an enlightened being?" The answer His Holiness gave was, "I am only a simple monk." Although His Holiness is a living Buddha, proclaiming his enlightenment would have been arrogant. Instead, the answer he gave was to show us that the more simple the mind, the easier our journey to enlightenment. Tara realized that the simple animal mind was the answer. Her deep relationships with many wild animals gave her the clue she was seeking and she shares it with you in this introductory book.

FREE THE MIND...FOR THOSE WHO ARE TRULY READY is the sequel to this book and is in the process of being written.

Made in United States
North Haven, CT
11 June 2025

69712249R00124